One-Minute Devotions

Morning by Morning

Charles H. Spurgeon

CHRISTIAN ART
Vereeniging

MORNING BY MORNING

© 1995 Christian Art, P.O. Box 1599, Vereeniging, South Africa

© All rights reserved.

Material in this book is adapted from *MORNING BY MORNING* and *EVENING BY EVENING*.

Printed in Singapore.

ISBN 1-86852-052-8

JANUARY

JANUARY 1

That year they ate of the produce of Canaan.
Joshua 5:12

Perhaps this year, you may rest in Christ. Our "promised rest" is to be with Jesus. If we are living by faith, that prospect should fill us with joy. As Paul says in Hebrews, "Now we who have believed enter that rest" (Hebrews 4:3).

JANUARY 2

Devote yourselves to prayer.
Colossians 4:2

A prayerless soul is a Christless soul. Prayer is the lisping of the believing infant, the shout of the fighting believer, the requiem of the dying saint falling asleep in Jesus. It is the breath, the watchword, the comfort, the strength, the honor of a Christian. If you are God's child, you will seek your Father's face and live in your Father's love.

JANUARY 3

I ... will make you to be a covenant for the people.
Isaiah 49:8

Believer, God's acceptance of Christ is your acceptance. Don't you know that the love the Father bestowed on Christ he is bestowing on you now? For all that Christ did is yours, perfect righteousness is yours; it is credited to your account. Christ is in the covenant.

JANUARY 4

But grow in the grace and knowledge of our Lord and Savior Jesus Christ.
2 Peter 3:18

Grow in grace – we should be growing in every aspect of our Lord's grace. That means growing in *faith*, in *love*, in *humility* as well. Try to lie very low, learning more about your own nothingness. As you grow downward in humility seek also to grow upward, growing closer to God in prayer.

JANUARY 5

God saw that the light was good, and he separated the light from the darkness.
Genesis 1:4

When the Holy Spirit gives us *spiritual* light, opening our eyes to behold the glory of God in the face of Jesus Christ, we see sin in its true colors and ourselves in our real position. O Lord Jesus, be our light throughout this whole day.

JANUARY 6

*Cast all your anxiety on
him because he cares for you.
1 Peter 5:7*

Christian, how can you dishonor your faith by looking so worried all the time? Cast your burden upon your Lord. Your heavenly Father would not even feel the weight that makes you stagger. Your crushing burden would be his speck of dust. Leave your concerns in the hands of a gracious God.

JANUARY 7

For to me, to live is Christ.
Philippians 1:21

A person begins to live for Christ when the Holy Spirit convinces him of his sin and when by grace he sees the Savior's sacrifice cleansing his guilt. For believers, Jesus is the "pearl of great price" (Matthew 13:45-46), for whom we are willing to part with all we have.

JANUARY 8

*He will bear the guilt
involved in the sacred gifts.
Exodus 28:38*

These words reveal a great deal. We should pause a while to reflect on this sad sight. The "guilt" involved in our public worship – the hypocrisy, formality. Or consider our work for the Lord – its selfishness, carelessness. Or our private devotions – their laxity, coldness, neglect. Yes, our "sacred gifts" contain far more guilt than we would think.

JANUARY 9

I will be their God.
Jeremiah 31:33

Christian, here is all you need. You want something that satisfies; isn't this enough? If you could pour this promise into a cup, wouldn't you say with David, "My cup overflows" (Psalm 23:5)? If God is your God, don't you have everything? If all else should fail, isn't his all-sufficiency enough to satisfy you?

JANUARY 10

*Now there is in store for me a
crown of righteousness.
2 Timothy 4:8*

If you believe in the Lord Jesus, if you have repented of sin and have a renewed heart, you are one of the Lord's people. There is a place reserved for you, a crown set aside, a harp ready for you to play.

JANUARY 11

They have no root.
Luke 8:13

Is this my case? Have I been putting on a good show on the outside, without any true life on the inside? Good growth takes place upward and downward at the same time. Am I rooted in sincere faith and love for Jesus? I don't want a godliness that sprouts up like Jonah's gourd (Jonah 4), but doesn't last. Let me count the cost of following Jesus. Let me feel the energy of his Holy Spirit. Then I will have a thriving *and lasting* seed in my soul.

JANUARY 12

And you are of Christ.
1 Corinthians 3:23

Show the world that you are the servant, the friend, the bride of Jesus. When you are tempted to sin, say, "I can't do this sinful thing, because I belong to Christ." It just does not make sense for a friend of Christ to sin. If you have professed faith in Christ, that is your profession. Act like a Christian. Let the way you talk make people think of Christ. Let them recognize his love and holiness in you, because you are of Christ.

JANUARY 13

Now Jehoshaphat built a fleet of trading ships to go to Ophir for gold, but they never set sail – they were wrecked at Ezion Geber.
1 Kings 22:48

May we have the grace to praise God not only for the shiploads of blessings he gives us, but also for the ships broken at Ezion Geber. We should not envy the more successful. Nor should we complain about our losses, as if we were the only ones who suffered misfortunes. This king's experience should serve as a warning to the rest of God's people.

JANUARY 14

Mighty to save.
Isaiah 63:1

Christ is not only "mighty to save" those who repent, but he is able to make people repent. Christ is mighty enough to make the man who hates holiness love it. He can make the woman who despises his name bend her knee before him. Christ does not bring a person to repentance and then let him shift for himself. He who begins the work carries it on (Philippians 1:6).

JANUARY 15

Do as you promised.
2 Samuel 7:25

When a Christian grasps a promise, if he does not take it to God, he dishonors him. But when he rushes to the throne of grace and cries, "This is all I have to stand on – your promise," then his desire is granted. Does the fountain get tired of flowing? No. God loves to hear the requests of needy souls. It is his nature to keep his promises. He delights in giving out favors. He is more ready to hear than you are to ask.

JANUARY 16

*"I myself will help you,"
declares the Lord.
Isaiah 41:14*

"Helping you is the least of the things I do for you. I have done far more – and I will continue to do more. Before the world began, I chose you. I made a covenant for you. I laid aside my glory and became a man for you. I gave my life for you. And if I did all this, I will surely help you now."

JANUARY 17

Then I looked, and there before me was the Lamb, standing on Mount Zion. Rev. 14:1

The major object of contemplation in the heavenly city is "the Lamb of God, who takes away the sin of the world" (John 1:29). That's what captured John's attention. Nothing else was as important as that Divine Being, who redeemed us by his blood. It is a joyous experience to have daily fellowship with Jesus. We will have the same joy in heaven, but to a higher degree. We will enjoy the constant vision of his presence. We will live with him forever.

JANUARY 18

There remains, then, a Sabbath-rest for the people of God.
Hebrews 4:9

Here, our rest is partial. There, it is perfect. Here, we remain unsettled; we feel there is always so much more to do. Think of that, if you are weary from your labors. Think of that eternal rest. Can you even imagine it? It is a rest that "remains". Here on earth, my best joys are mortal. My fairest flowers fade. My sweetest birds fall to death's arrows. My most pleasant days are shadowed into nights.

JANUARY 19

I looked for him but did not find him. Song of Songs 3:1

Tell me where you lost track of Christ, and I will tell you where you will probably find him. Did you lose him in the prayer closet by neglecting regular prayer? Did you lose Christ when you turned to sin? Did you lose Christ by neglecting the Scriptures? It is easier to go twenty miles forward than to go one mile back to retrieve something you have lost. Seek him with your whole heart, and you will find him. Give yourself thoroughly to this search, and once again he will be your joy and gladness.

JANUARY 20

Now Abel kept flocks.
Genesis 4:2

Abel, the shepherd, offered a sacrifice of blood, dedicating it to God. Abel was hated by his brother, hated without cause. So was our Savior. It is a very precious thing to stand at the altar of our Good Shepherd, to see him bleeding there as a slaughtered priest, and then to hear his blood speaking peace to his whole flock. He speaks peace to our consciences, peace between Jew and Gentile, peace between God and humanity, peace throughout eternity for blood-washed souls.

JANUARY 21

And so all Israel will be saved.
Romans 11:26

When Moses sang at the Red Sea, it was his joy to know that *all* Israel was safe. And at the end of time, when all God's chosen ones will sing the song of Moses and of the Lamb, this will be the boast of Jesus – "None has been lost" (John 17:12). There will be no vacant thrones in heaven. All the ones God has chosen, all those redeemed by Christ, all those the Spirit has called, all who believe in Jesus, will safely cross the dividing sea.

JANUARY 22

Son of man, how is the wood of a vine better than that of a branch on any of the trees in the forest?
Ezekiel 15:2

The Lord strung these vines on the walls of his sanctuary, and they bear fruit for his glory. But what are they without God? What are they without the continual influence of the Spirit, making them fruitful? Get rid of pride, believer. You have no reason for it. If you amount to anything right now, it is because of God's grace. That's what makes you different from anyone else.

JANUARY 23

*I have exalted a young man
from among the people.
Psalm 89:19*

Remember this, Christian, and let it comfort you. However difficult and painful your road may be, it is marked by the footsteps of the Savior. Even when you reach the dark valley of the shadow of death and the deep waters of the surging Jordan, you will find his footprints there. Wherever you go, he has gone. Each burden we have to carry has at one time been laid on the shoulders of Immanuel.

JANUARY 24

*Surely he will save you
from the fowler's snare.
Psalm 91:3*

How does God save us from the snare? He often uses trouble. God knows that our backsliding leads to our destruction. In mercy, he sends the rod of affliction. We say, "Why, Lord?" Not knowing that our trouble has been God's way of protecting us from a far greater evil. But you say you cannot return; you are a captive. Then listen again to this promise – "Surely he will save you from the fowler's snare."

JANUARY 25

*I will tell of the kindnesses
of the Lord ...
Isaiah 63:7*

What kindnesses have you experienced? Have you never been helped in a time of need? I know you have. Go back, then, to the choice mercies of yesterday. It may be dark now, but if you light up the lamps of the past, they will glitter through the darkness. They will help you trust in the Lord until the day breaks and the shadows flee.

JANUARY 26

Your heavenly Father.
Matthew 6:26

Father! Oh, what a precious word that is! Here is authority. Because he is our Father, we owe him obedience. The obedience that God's children show him must be loving obedience. Don't go about God's service as slaves might go about their taskmaster's toil. Enjoy it, because it is your Father's desire. *Father!* Here we find honor and love. How great is a father's love for his children! It goes beyond friendship.

JANUARY 27

*From the fullness of his grace
we have all received one
blessing after another.
John 1:16*

There is a fullness of blessings of every sort and shape – a fullness of grace to forgive us, to make us new, to make us holy, to keep us safe, to make us more like Christ. Come, believer, get all your need supplied. Ask for much, and you will get much. This fullness is inexhaustible, and it is stored up where all the needy may reach it – in Jesus.

JANUARY 28

Perfect in Christ.
Colossians 1:28

You are not perfect. You know that in your soul. You know your heart too well to even dream for a moment of any perfection *in yourself*. But in the middle of this sad situation, there is comfort for you – you are "perfect *in Christ*". In God's sight, you are "complete in him". Right now, you stand accepted by God.

JANUARY 29

We fix our eyes not on what is seen, but on what is unseen.
2 Corinthians 4:18

In our Christian pilgrimage, it is good to look forward. Our crown is in front of us, our goal lies ahead. Looking ahead with the eyes of faith, we see the hope, joy, comfort, and inspiration of the future. We see sin cast out, the body of sin and death destroyed, the soul made perfect. We see ourselves as partakers of the inheritance of the saints.

JANUARY 30

As soon as you hear the sound of marching in the tops of the balsam trees, move quickly.
2 Samuel 5:24

There are times when the "sound of marching" is heard in your personal life. You become especially powerful in prayer. The Spirit gives you joy and gladness. The Scripture is open to you, and you apply its promises. Now is the time to "move quickly". Get rid of some evil habit. Develop new habits of prayer in this time when you feel close to Christ.

JANUARY 31

The Lord Our Righteousness.
Jeremiah 23:6

Though distress may afflict me, though Satan assaults me, I can rest in the fact that Christ has made me righteous. On the cross he said, "It is finished!" If it is finished, then I am complete in him. and I can rejoice – "not having a righteousness of my own that comes from the law, but that which is through faith in Christ" (Philippians 3:9).

FEBRUARY

FEBRUARY 1

*May they sing of the
ways of the Lord.
Psalm 138:5*

Do you recall the day when your fetters fell off? Do you remember the place where Jesus met you and said, "I have loved you with an everlasting love?" Oh, what a great time that is, when Jesus takes away the pain of sin. As long as they live, Christians keep discovering reasons to sing of the ways of the Lord. Their daily experience makes them say, "I will extol the Lord at all time; his praise will always be on my lips."

FEBRUARY 2

Without the shedding of blood there is no forgiveness.
Hebrews 9:22

This is an eternal truth. Sin cannot be pardoned without atonement. That means that there is no hope for me outside of Christ, for there is no other blood that can truly take away my sin. Sin will yield to nothing less powerful than the blood of the Savior. We should be glad that we have a way to be forgiven! Why go looking for another?

FEBRUARY 3

*Therefore, brethren,
we are debtors.
Romans 8:12 KJV*

Christ said, "It is finished!" Whatever his people owed was wiped from the books. Christ has satisfied the divine justice. The account is settled. The bill has been nailed to the cross. The receipt has been given. But then, because we are not debtors anymore in *that* sense, we become ten times more God's debtors in another sense. Pause and ponder for a moment. Think about how much you owe to God's sovereignty, to his forgiving grace.

FEBRUARY 4

As the Lord loves the Israelites.
Hosea 3:1

When you enter the mysteries of eternity, there will be no need to tremble. "For I am convinced that neither death nor life, neither angels nor demons, neither the present nor the future, nor any powers, neither height nor depth, nor anything else in all creation, will be able to separate us from the love of God that is in Christ Jesus our Lord" (Romans 8:38-39).

FEBRUARY 5

The Father has sent his Son to be the Savior of the world.
1 John 4:14

Meditate on this today. The *Father* sent him! Jesus does what the Father plans. In the wounds of the dying Savior, see the love of the great I AM. Every time you think of Jesus, think of the eternal loving Father who sent him.

FEBRUARY 6

*And pray in the Spirit
on all occasions.
Ephesians 6:18*

We have prayed for grace to help us live holy lives, for a fresh assurance of our salvation, for the application of God's promises, for deliverance from temptation, for strength to do God's work, for comfort in times of testing. We are like beggars, regularly approaching God to ask for whatever our souls need. Remember this, and let it fill your heart with gratitude.

FEBRUARY 7

*Get up, go away! For this
is not your resting place.
Micah 2:10*

All of us will hear this message sooner or later. "Get up! It's time to leave your home, your business, your family, and your friends. It is time to take your final journey." This will be our last move. We will live forever with the Lord we love and with all his people. Christian, meditate on heaven as much as you can; it will help you to press on, to forget how difficult the journey can be.

FEBRUARY 8

*You are to give him
the name Jesus.
Matthew 1:21*

If there is one name sweeter than any other, it is the name *Jesus*. Jesus! It is the name that moves the harps of heaven to make beautiful melody. Jesus! It is woven into the very fabric of our worship. Many of our hymns begin with it, and hardly any, if they're worth anything, end without mentioning it. It is the sum total of all delights. It gathers up all the hallelujahs of eternity in just five letters. Jesus!

FEBRUARY 9

So David inquired of the Lord.
2 Samuel 5:23

Learn this from David. Take no step without God. If you want to stay on the right path, let God be your compass. If you want to steer your ship safely through the storm, let God's hand rest on the tiller. We will avoid many rocks, many shoals and quicksands, if we let our Father take the helm. We must let God's providence lead the way. "I will instruct you and teach you in the way you should go" (Psalm 32:8).

FEBRUARY 10

I know how to abound.
Philippians 4:12 KJV

The Christian is more apt to disgrace his faith in prosperity than in adversity. It is a dangerous thing to be prosperous. The material bounty that God gives us often leads us to neglect spiritual things. Our souls grow lean as our bodies grow fat. Because of our pride and forgetfulness, prosperity is difficult for us. So be sure to ask God to teach you how to abound.

FEBRUARY 11

They took note that these men had been with Jesus.
Acts 4:13

A Christian should be a striking likeness of Jesus Christ. Imitate Jesus in his *holiness*. He was zealous; you should be, too, always going about doing good. He was self-denying; you should be, too. He was devout; you, too, should be fervent in your prayers. He submitted to his Father's will; and so should you. He was patient; and you, too, must learn to endure. Above all, try to forgive your enemies, as Jesus did.

FEBRUARY 12

For just as the sufferings of Christ flow over into our lives, so also through Christ our comfort overflows.
2 Corinthians 1:5

The Ruler of All holds a set of scales. In one side he puts his people's trials. In the other he puts their comforts. Why? For one thing, *trials make more room for comfort*. Another reason is this. When we have troubles, *we have our closest dealings with God*. So do not fret over your heavy troubles. They are the heralds of great mercies.

FEBRUARY 13

Dear friends, now we are children of God.
1 John 3:2

When we consider the kind of people we were and how corrupt we still feel sometimes, this adoption is truly amazing. We are the children of God! What an honored relationship this is, and what privileges it brings! What care and tenderness the child expects from his father, and what love a father feels toward his child! All of that – and more – we now have through Christ.

FEBRUARY 14

Day by day the king gave Jehoiachin a regular allowance as long as he lived.
2 Kings 25:30

The conquered King Jehoiachin was released from prison and treated with honor. But he was not given provisions to last for months. He was given a daily allowance. In this, he models the ideal position of all God's people. We cannot eat or drink or wear more than one day's supply of food and clothing. When our Father does not give us more, we should be content with his daily allowance.

FEBRUARY 15

*To him be glory both
now and forever.
2 Peter 3:18*

Why not make this your prayer today? "Lord, help me to glorify you. I am poor, but help me to glorify you by being content. I am sick, but help me to honor you with my patience. I have talents; help me to use them for you. You have put me in the world for something, Lord. Show me what that is. I am yours. Take me, and show me how to glorify you *now*."

FEBRUARY 16

*I have learned to be content
whatever the circumstances.
Philippians 4:11*

Contentment is not a natural propensity of man. But the precious things of the earth must be cultivated. If we want flowers, we must garden. Now contentment is one of the flowers of heaven. If we want it, we must cultivate it. It will not grow naturally. Only the new nature can produce it, and even then we must take special care of the grace God has planted inside us.

FEBRUARY 17

Isaac ... lived near Beer Lahai Roi.
Genesis 25:11

Hagar had met the angel of God at the well called Beer Lahai Roi. The name means "the well of the Living One who sees me". The seeing God met their needs. Isaac *lived* there. He made the well of the living and all-seeing God the source of his livelihood. This is the true test of a person – where does his soul *live?*

FEBRUARY 18

*Tell me what charges
you have against me.
Job 10:2*

Are you being tested like Job? Perhaps the Lord is trying to develop some aspects of your character — faith, love, and hope. Hard times are often the dark background against which God sets the jewels of his children's faith, hope, and love — they shine all the brighter. Isn't God helping you to grow?

FEBRUARY 19

Once again I will yield to the plea of the house of Israel and do this for them.
Ezekiel 36:37

Prayer is the forerunner of mercy. Search through sacred history, and you will find that hardly ever did a great mercy come to this world without prayer paving its way. Prayer led to new assurance. As you think about the great joys of your life, you have to see them as answers to prayer. The things we ask for are precious, but we do not realize how precious until we have earnestly asked God for them.

FEBRUARY 20

*But God, who comforts
the downcast.
2 Corinthians 7:6*

So Christian, when you are dry, go to God. Ask him to dowse your soul with joy. Then your joy will be full. Don't go to earthly friends. But go first and foremost to the God who comforts the downcast, and you will soon find yourself saying, "When anxiety was great within me, your consolation brought joy to my soul" (Psalm 94:19).

FEBRUARY 21

God has said.
Hebrews 13:5

There may be a promise in God's Word that would fit your situation exactly, but you may not know of it, so you miss out on its comfort. You are like a prisoner in a dungeon, with a ring of keys. One of the keys would unlock the door and free you. But if you don't look for it, you will remain a prisoner, though your liberty is so close at hand. There may be a powerful medicine in Scripture's pharmacy. But you will remain sick until you search for what "God has said".

FEBRUARY 22

*But his bow remained steady,
his strong arms stayed limber,
because of the hand of the
Mighty One of Jacob.
Genesis 49:24*

Why did Joseph resist temptation? God helped him. We can do nothing without God's power. All true strength comes from "the Mighty One of Jacob".

FEBRUARY 23

Never will I leave you.
Hebrews 13:5

Be bold to believe, because he has said; "Never will I leave *you*, never will I forsake *you*." In this promise, God gives his people everything. Suddenly all the attributes of God are there for our use. Is he mighty? He shows his strength on behalf of those who trust him. Everything living or dying, in this world or the next, now and on the resurrection morning – it is all here for you. God tells you, "Never will I leave you."

FEBRUARY 24

I will send down showers in season; there will be showers of blessing.
Ezekiel 34:26

God's grace, like rain, is also *seasonable*. It comes at the right time. What is your season this morning? Are you in a drought? Then that is the season for God's showers. Is it a season of weariness and dark clouds? Then that is the time for God's blessing. Look up today, O parched plant, and open your leaves and flowers for a heavenly watering.

FEBRUARY 25

The coming wrath.
Matthew 3:7

God's hand of mercy is now outstretched, offering to lead you to Christ. He will shelter you from the storm. You know you need him. Believe in him, throw yourself upon his mercy, and let the approaching storm of God's wrath blow over you.

FEBRUARY 26

Salvation comes from the Lord.
Jonah 2:9

Salvation is the work of God. Only he can bring life to the soul that is "dead in ... transgressions and sins". Without Jesus I can do nothing. As a branch cannot bear fruit unless it remains in the vine (John 15:4), neither can I, unless I remain in Jesus.

FEBRUARY 27

*If you make the Most
High your dwelling – even
the Lord, who is my refuge.
Psalm 91:9*

Let all my prospects fall through; let my hopes be blasted; let my joy wither – I will never lose what I have in God. He is my safe dwelling place. I am a pilgrim in this world, but at home with God. On the earth I wander, but in God I live in peace.

FEBRUARY 28

My hope comes from him.
Psalm 62:5

If we are looking for any satisfaction from this world, our hopes will be dashed. But if we look to God to supply our wants, both temporal and spiritual, we will be satisfied. My Lord never fails to honor his promises. When we bring them to his throne, he never sends them back unanswered. Therefore, I will wait, hat in hand, only at his door.

FEBRUARY 29

*I have drawn you
with loving-kindness.
Jeremiah 31:3*

God uses the thunders of the law and the terrors of judgment to bring us to Christ. But he wins his final victory with loving-kindness. In every case, loving-kindness wins the day. What Moses could never do with his tablets of stone, Christ does with his wounded hand.

MARCH

MARCH 1

Awake, north wind, and come, south wind! Blow on my garden, that its fragrance may spread abroad.
Song of Songs 4:16

Those Christian virtues that we do not exercise are like the fragrant nectar that stays slumbering in the cups of the flowers. Yet when our wise Gardener allows the winds of both affliction and comfort to blow on us, these winds catch our aromas of faith, love, patience, hope, resignation, joy, and so on, spreading them far and wide.

MARCH 2

So all Israel went down to the Philistines to have their plowshares, mattocks, axes and sickles sharpened.
1 Samuel 13:20

Most of our tools need sharpening. We need quickness of perception, tact, energy, promptness – we must adapt everything for the Lord's work. Practical common sense is scarce among Christians. We should learn from our enemies how to bless, not curse, and how to truly serve our true Lord.

MARCH 3

I have chosen thee in the furnace of affliction.
Isaiah 48:10 KJV

Don't be afraid, Christian, Jesus is with you. In all your fiery trials, his presence is both your comfort and safety. He will never leave one whom he has chosen as his own. So take hold of him and follow where he leads. "So do not fear, for I am with you; do not be dismayed, for I am your God" (Isaiah 41:10).

MARCH 4

My grace is sufficient for you.
2 Corinthians 12:9

He who wants to glorify God can count on facing many trials. No one can truly shine for Christ without enduring many conflicts. So if you have a difficult path, rejoice in it. You are demonstrating the all-sufficient grace of God. The God who has been sufficient until now should be trusted to the end.

MARCH 5

*Let us not be like others,
who are asleep.
1 Thessalonians 5:6*

Christians who isolate themselves and walk alone are liable to grow drowsy. Join with other Christians, though, and you will stay awake, refreshed, encouraged, and will make quicker progress on the road to heaven. But as you converse with other believers, make sure that your theme is Jesus. My friend, live close to the cross, and you will not sleep.

MARCH 6

You must be born again.
John 3:7

This great work of rebirth is *supernatural*. A person cannot do this by himself. God infuses a whole new principle in a person's heart, renewing the soul, affecting one's entire life. It is not a change of my name, but a renewal of my nature. I am not the man I used to be, but a new man in Christ Jesus.

MARCH 7

Have faith in God.
Mark 11:22

Faith gives feet to the soul. With faith, the soul can march along the road of God's commandments. Love can make the feet move more swiftly, but faith *is* both feet. Faith is the oil that enables the wheels of holy devotion and earnest piety to move well. Without faith, the wheels grind to a halt.

MARCH 8

We must go through many hardships to enter the kingdom of God.
Acts 14:22

But although tribulation is the path of God's children, they have the comfort of knowing that their Master has walked this path first. They have his presence and sympathy to cheer them, his grace to support them, and his example to guide them. And when they reach his kingdom, it will be worth it all.

MARCH 9

He is altogether lovely.
Song of Songs 5:16

All earthly suns have their spots. Even our beautiful earth has its deserts. As much as we may love any earthly thing, we cannot love every part of it. But Christ Jesus is the purest gold, light without darkness, bright glory unclouded. He is *altogether* lovely.

MARCH 10

When I felt secure, I said,
"I will never be shaken."
Psalm 30:6

Brother or sister, beware of the smooth places along the way. When the way is rough, thank God for it. If God always rocked us in the cradle of prosperity, if there were never any bitter drops in the wine of this life, we would become intoxicated with pleasure. Let us bless God, then, for our afflictions. Let us thank him for our changes.

MARCH 11

*So that ... sin might
become utterly sinful.
Romans 7:13*

Christian, beware of this. By thinking lightly of sin, you may be falling little by little. This "little" thing of sin circled our Savior's head with thorns: it made him suffer anguish. Look on all sin as that which crucified the Savior, and you, too, will see that it is "utterly sinful".

MARCH 12

Love your neighbor.
Matthew 5:43

Perhaps you are saying, "I'd like to love my neighbors, but whenever I do anything, they return ingratitude and contempt." Well, that gives you more opportunity for the heroism of love. Love is no feather bed; it's a battle. The one who dares the most will win the most. Love your neighbor, for in that way you are following the footsteps of Christ.

MARCH 13

Why stay here until we die?
2 Kings 7:3

If you seek the Lord, you will find him. Jesus turns away no one who comes to him. You will not perish if you trust him. I pray that the Holy Spirit will embolden you to get up and go to Jesus. It will not be in vain. When you yourself are saved, broadcast the good news to others. Don't hold back.

MARCH 14

So, if you think you are standing firm, be careful that you don't fall!
1 Corinthians 10:12

It is a curious fact that there is such a thing as being proud of grace. Someone may say, "I have great faith. I will never fall." But he who boasts of grace has little grace to boast of. It makes no sense to glory in your own faith and love. Let your confidence be in Christ and his strength. Only he can keep you from falling.

MARCH 15

*Be strong in the grace
that is in Christ Jesus.
2 Timothy 2:1*

Grace, whether its work is to pardon, to cleanse, to preserve, to strengthen, to enlighten, to bring to life, or to restore – grace is always available from him freely and without price. Day by day we receive grace from Jesus. As we learn to recognize that this grace comes from him, we will sense our communion with him and enjoy this fellowship all the more.

MARCH 16

*I dwell with you as an
alien, a stranger.
Psalm 39:12*

Now, in fellowship with you, I walk through this sinful world as a pilgrim in a foreign country. *You* are a stranger in your own world, Lord. People forget you, dishonor you, set up new laws and strange customs, and do not recognize you. Lord, I don't want to be a citizen in a world where Jesus was a stranger. His pierced hands have loosened the cords that used to bind my soul to this earth. Now I, too, am a stranger here.

MARCH 17

Remember the poor.
Galatians 2:10

Why does God allow so many of his children to be poor? There are many reasons. For one, he wants to give those of us who have enough an opportunity to show our love for Jesus. He wants us to show our love not only in our words, but also by our actions. Everything we do for God's needy people is accepted by Christ as a gift for himself.

MARCH 18

You are all sons of God through faith in Christ Jesus.
Galatians 3:26

Listen, you are just as much a child of God as the person with great faith. Peter and Paul, those highly favored apostles, were members of God's family – and so are you. A weak Christian belongs to this family just as much as a strong one. This thought should comfort us as we come to God in prayer, saying, "Our Father."

MARCH 19

Strengthened in his faith.
Romans 4:20

Faith links me with God. Faith clothes me with his power. Faith puts the divine power at my disposal. Faith calls every attribute of God to my defense. It helps me defeat the hosts of hell. With faith, I march in triumph over my enemies. But without faith, how can I receive anything from the Lord?

MARCH 20

My beloved!
Song of Songs 2:8 KJV

He is very precious to us, "outstanding among ten thousand ... altogether lovely" (Song of Songs 5:10, 16). The love between Jesus and the church is so strong that the apostle dares to defy the whole universe to separate her from Christ's love. Persecutions cannot do this. "No," he boasts, "in all these things we are more than conquerors through him who loved us" (Romans 8:35, 37).

MARCH 21

You will be scattered ... You will leave me all alone.
John 16:32

Few knew the sorrows of Gethsemane. Most of Jesus' followers were not sufficiently advanced in grace to be allowed to witness the mysteries of Christ's agony. Only Peter, James, and John could approach the veil of our Lord's mysterious sorrow. They were left a stone's throw away. Jesus had to go through this experience alone. Isaac Watts is right when he sings, "All the unknown joys he gives, were bought with agonies unknown."

MARCH 22

Going a little farther, he fell with his face to the ground and prayed.
Matthew 26:39

First, it was *lonely* prayer. He withdrew even from his three favorite disciples. It was *humble* prayer. Luke says he knelt, but Matthew adds that he "fell with his face to the ground". It was *filial* prayer. That is, he was praying as a Son to his Father. Note that it was also *persevering* prayer. He prayed three times. It was also a prayer of *resignation*. "Yet not as I will," he prayed, "but as you will." Yield to God, and he yields to you.

MARCH 23

His sweat was like drops of blood falling to the ground.
Luke 22:44

The mental pressure arising from our Lord's struggle with temptation forced him into such a state that his pores exuded great drops of blood. This shows how great the weight of sin must have been. It was already crushing our Lord.

MARCH 24

*He was heard because of his
reverent submission.
Hebrews 5:7*

Jesus had a choice as he prayed in the garden: fear the Lord and yield in obedience to him or fear everything else that Satan might throw at him. He chose to fear the Lord, in reverent submission. So should we.

MARCH 25

*The kisses of an enemy are deceitful.
Proverbs 27:6 KJV*

Whenever someone is about to stab religion, he usually professes great reverence for it. Beware of the sleek-faced hypocrisy that brings heresy right behind it. Do I live in the world as carelessly as others do and yet profess to follow Jesus? O Lord, keep me clear in this matter. Make me sincere and true.

MARCH 26

*If you are looking for me,
then let these men go.
John 18:8*

See how much care Jesus showed for his disciples even in his hour of trial. Jesus surrenders himself to the enemy but speaks forcefully to set his friends free. For himself, "as a sheep before her shearers is silent, so he did not open his mouth." But for his disciples' sake he speaks with Almighty energy. Here is love – constant, self-forgetting, faithful love.

MARCH 27

*Then all the disciples
deserted him and fled.
Matthew 26:56*

He never deserted them. But they, fearing for their lives, fled from him as his sufferings just began. This is just one example of how frail we believers are on our own. At best, we are sheep – and we run off when the wolf comes. Yet God's grace can make the coward brave. And the Holy Spirit can make my timid spirit brave enough to confess my allegiance to the Lord.

MARCH 28

This love that surpasses knowledge. Ephesians 3:19

To begin to get an idea of Jesus' love, we must understand the glory he came from – and how far he came to pour himself out in shame upon the earth. To bleed, to die, to suffer – these were unthinkable for the very Son of God. To suffer such unparalleled agony – this is a depth of love our minds cannot begin to grasp. This is love. Love that "surpasses knowledge". Let this love fill your heart with adoring gratitude and lead you to some practical manifestations of its power.

MARCH 29

Although he was a son, he learned obedience from what he suffered.
Hebrews 5:8

The Captain of our salvation was "made perfect" through suffering. The true-born child of God should not try to escape it – even if he could. But there is one very comforting thought in the fact of Christ's being "made perfect through suffering". He can sympathize fully with us. Believer, grab onto this thought in your times of agony. Let the thought of Jesus strengthen you as you follow in his steps.

MARCH 30

*He ... was numbered with
the transgressors.
Isaiah 53:12*

Why did Jesus allow himself to be counted among sinners? There were many reasons. First, by doing so, he could better serve as their advocate. Our Lord Jesus was also numbered with the transgressors so that their hearts might be drawn toward him. Wasn't Jesus also listed on the roll of sinners so that we might be listed in the roll of saints? Jesus has taken our situation upon himself, and all that Jesus possesses is now ours.

MARCH 31

By his wounds we are healed.
Isaiah 53:5

Pilate handed Jesus over to his soldiers to be scourged. He had been beaten before, but this Roman scourging was probably the most severe. We may weep as we imagine the blows upon his precious body. Jesus stands before you, believer, as a mirror of agonizing love. If we have ever loved our Lord Jesus, that love must be growing now as we consider his agony – the pain he went through for us.

APRIL

APRIL 1

*Let him kiss me with
the kisses of his mouth.
Song of Songs 1:2*

We walk by faith, but we rest in Christ's fellowship. Faith is the road, but communion with Jesus is the well from which we drink. O lover of our souls, come close to us. Let the lips of your blessing meet the lips of our asking. Let the lips of your fullness touch the lips of our need.

APRIL 2

But Jesus made no reply, not even to a single charge.
Matthew 27:14

Jesus had never been slow to speak when he was blessing others, but here he does not say a word in his own defense. This silence shows us the nature of *his perfect self-sacrifice*. By his silence, Jesus also demonstrated *the best reply to a hostile world*. Calm endurance answers some questions far more conclusively than the loftiest eloquence. Be with us, Jesus, and in the silence of our hearts, let us hear the voice of your love.

APRIL 3

*So the soldiers took
charge of Jesus.
John 19:16*

He had been hurried from Caiaphas to Pilate, from Pilate to Herod, and from Herod back again to Pilate. They were eager for his blood and therefore led him out to die, weighed down with the cross. As you see this scene, weep with the daughters of Jerusalem. Don't let this picture vanish until you have rejoiced in your own deliverance and adored the loving Redeemer who took your sins upon himself.

APRIL 4

God made him who had no sin to be sin for us, so that in him we might become the righteousness of God.
2 Corinthians 5:21

Do you feel guilty about your sinfulness? Look to your perfect Lord and remember: You are complete in him. You know that someday you will stand before God's throne, and he will declare you righteous through Christ. But you are accepted just as thoroughly *today*, even with all your sinfulness. Grab on to this thought: You are perfect in Christ. Wearing his garment, you are as holy as the Holy One.

APRIL 5

They seized Simon ... and put the cross on him and made him carry it behind Jesus.
Luke 23:26

We see here a picture of the church: She follows Jesus, bearing the cross. Note that Jesus did not suffer to keep you from suffering. He bears the cross not for you to escape it, but for you to endure it. But we can comfort ourselves with this thought: As with Simon, it is not our cross, but Christ's cross that we carry. When you are mocked for your devotion to Jesus, remember it is *his* cross.

APRIL 6

*Let us, then, go to him
outside the camp.
Hebrews 13:13*

In the same way, Christ's people must "go to him outside the camp". We must be prepared to tread the straight and narrow path. We must have bold, unflinching, lionlike hearts, loving Christ and his truth far more than we love the world. You cannot grow very much in grace while you are conformed to the world. The life of separation may be a path of sorrow, but it is the highway of safety.

APRIL 7

How long, O men, will you turn my glory into shame?
Psalm 4:2

One writer has noted the mocking "honors" that the blinded people of Israel gave to Jesus, their King. He was provided with a *guard of honor*, who showed their esteem by gambling over his garments. A *throne of honor* was found for him on the bloody tree. The *title of honor* was written as "King of the Jews". In each case, men turned Jesus' glory into shame, but it eternally gladdens the eyes of saints and angels.

APRIL 8

For if men do these things when the tree is green, what will happen when it is dry?
Luke 23:31

There are many interpretations for this intriguing question. Here is a good one. "If I, the innocent substitute for sinners, suffer like this, what will happen when the sinner himself – the dry tree – falls into the hands of an angry God?" We cannot sum up in one word all the sorrows that came upon Jesus. So it is impossible to say what streams, what oceans of grief must come upon your soul if you die without Christ.

APRIL 9

A large number of people followed him, including women who mourned and wailed for him.
Luke 23:27

Those women had their reasons to love Christ and weep, but so do I. Perhaps one was the widow of Nain, who saw her son brought back to life. But I have also been raised to newness of life. Perhaps another was Peter's mother-in-law, cured of a fever. But I have been cured of a greater disease: sin itself. So since I owe as much to my Savior as these women did, let me join them in gratitude and grief.

APRIL 10

The place, which is called Calvary.
Luke 23:33 KJV

Calvary is the hill of our comfort. The house of our consolation is built with the wood of the cross. The temple of heavenly blessing is founded on that riven rock – riven by the spear that pierced his side. No scene in sacred history gladdens the soul like Calvary's tragedy. So Calvary's comfort is rare and rich. We would never have known Christ's love in all its heights and depths if he had not died. If you want to know love, come to Calvary, and see the Man of Sorrows die.

APRIL 11

*I am poured out like water, and all
my bones are out of joint.
Psalm 22:14*

As we kneel before the throne of our ascended Savior, let us drink of the cup of his strength so that we may be ready for our time of trial. Every part of his body suffered, but he came through it all, into his power and glory, uninjured. Even so shall his spiritual body, the church, come through the furnace with not so much as the smell of fire upon it.

APRIL 12

My heart has turned to wax; it has melted away within me.
Psalm 22:14

Believer, come to the cross this morning and humbly adore the King of Glory. Realize that he was once brought far lower, in mental distress and inward anguish, than any of us. See how well he qualifies to be our High Priest – for he has felt our infirmities. Let that strong, deep love of Jesus flow into your soul like a stream flooding its banks. Let it flood all your faculties, drown all your sins, wash away your cares.

APRIL 13

My lover is to me a sachet of myrrh. Song of Songs 1:13

Why myrrh? It may be used here as a type of Jesus – but why a whole *sachet* of myrrh? First, the amount. He is not just a drop of myrrh; he's a whole bundle. There is enough in Christ for all my needs – I should not be slow to avail myself of this resource. Second, for variety. Christ does not only meet a single need, but "in Christ all the fullness of the Deity lives in bodily form". He gives his perfume only to those who enter into communion with him, who come close to his presence.

APRIL 14

All who see me mock me; they hurl insults, shaking their heads.
Psalm 22:7

Mockery was a major ingredient in our Lord's sorrows. Judas mocked him in the garden; the chief priests and scribes laughed him to scorn; Herod despised him; the servants and the soldiers jeered at him and brutally insulted him. O Jesus, "despised and rejected by men" (Isaiah 53:3), how could you die for people who treated you so poorly? Here is love amazing, love divine, yes, love beyond degree.

APRIL 15

My God, my God, why have you forsaken me?
Psalm 22:1

Here we see the Savior in the depth of his sorrows. With Christ, it was a *real* forsaking. In our case, our cries often come from unbelief. In Christ's case, it was a statement of dreadful fact – for God really had turned away from him. If you are a poor, distressed soul, who once lived in the sunshine of God's face, but are now in darkness, remember that he has not really forsaken you.

APRIL 16

The precious blood of Christ.
1 Peter 1:19

Standing at the foot of the cross, we see hands, feet, and side, all pouring out crimson streams of precious blood. Why is it "precious"? Because it *redeems* us. By this blood, the sins of Christ's people are atoned for. We are redeemed from under the law. We are reconciled to God, made one with him. The precious blood of Christ also *sanctifies* us. It not only takes away our sin, but also awakens our new nature and leads us on to follow God's commands.

APRIL 17

The sprinkled blood that speaks a better word than the blood of Abel.
Hebrews 12:24

Have you come to this sprinkled blood? I'm not asking whether you have come to a knowledge of doctrine or the observance of ceremonies or some special experience, but *have you come to the blood of Jesus?* To the repentant people of earth, the shedding of Christ's blood is the music of heaven. We are full of sin, but as we gaze on the Savior's wounds, each drop of blood, as it falls, cries, "It is finished! I have put an end to sin!"

APRIL 18

*And she tied the scarlet
cord in the window.
Joshua 2:21*

Rahab put her life in the hands of the spies. To her, they were representatives of the God of Israel. Her faith was simple and firm, but it was very obedient. Tying the scarlet cord in the window was a very trivial act in itself, but she dared not forget it. There is One who sees that scarlet line even when I lack the faith to see it myself. My Lord will see it and preserve me from his judgment.

APRIL 19

At that moment the curtain of the temple was torn in two from top to bottom.
Matthew 27:51

This was no small miracle – the tearing of such a thick veil – but it was not intended merely as a display of power. *Access to God is now available* to every believer in Christ Jesus. This is not some small peephole, through which we may peer at the mercy seat. No, this veil has been ripped apart, from top to bottom. We may come boldly to the throne of heavenly grace.

APRIL 20

So that by his death he might destroy him who holds the power of death.
Hebrews 2:14

Death has lost its sting, because the devil's power over it is destroyed. Then why are you afraid to die? Ask God to give you such a deep awareness of your Redeemer's death that you will be strengthened for that final hour. Living near the cross of Calvary, you may think of death with pleasure and welcome it with intense delight when it comes.

APRIL 21

I know that my Redeemer lives.
Job 19:25

The marrow of Job's comfort lies in that little word *my* – "*my* Redeemer" – and in the fact that his Redeemer *lives*. Oh, to get hold of a living Christ! Certainly if Job, in those ages before the coming of Christ, could say, "I know," we should not speak any less positively. A living Redeemer, truly mine, is joy unspeakable.

APRIL 22

God exalted him.
Acts 5:31

Jesus our Lord, once crucified, dead, and buried, now sits on the throne of glory. He has an undisputed right to the highest place that heaven affords. So be content to live unknown for now, and to walk your weary way through the fields of poverty or up the hills of affliction. Someday you will reign with Christ, for he has made us "kings and priests", and we will reign forever.

APRIL 23

No, in all these things we are more than conquerors through him who loved us.
Romans 8:37

We go to Christ for forgiveness, but all too often we look to the law for the power to fight our sins. Your prayers, your repentances, your tears – all of them put together – are worth nothing apart from him. You must be conquerors through him who has loved you, if you will be conquerors at all.

APRIL 24

And because of all this we make a sure covenant.
Nehemiah 9:38 KJV

We need to be reminded regularly of God's promises to us. In the same way, we should renew our old vows, praying for God's strength to be true to them. This is a good time now. For the last month we have been considering Christ's sufferings. With gratitude, then, let us renew our "sure covenant" with the Lord.

APRIL 25

Arise, my darling, my beautiful one, and come with me.
Song of Songs 2:10

"Come with me!" The sound is not harsh at all. What possible reason would I have for staying in this wilderness of vanity and sin? Lord, I want to come with you, but I am caught in these thorns and can't get away. If it were possible, I would like to have no heart for sin, no eyes or ears for sin. Draw me. Your grace can do it. Send your Spirit to kindle sacred flames of love in my heart.

APRIL 26

Do this in remembrance of me.
1 Corinthians 11:24

It would seem, from this verse, that Christians could forget Christ! How can those who have been redeemed by the blood of the dying Lamb and loved with an everlasting love ever forget their gracious Savior? Let's bind a heavenly forget-me-not around our hearts for Jesus, our Beloved. Whatever else we may forget, let's hold fast to him.

APRIL 27

God, our God, will bless us.
Psalm 67:6

It is strange how little use we make of the spiritual blessings God gives us, but stranger how little use we make of God himself. He is "our God", but we pay little attention to him and ask him few favors. Whatever you are, wherever you are, remember God is there when you need him; he is *what you need* and he is *everything* you need.

APRIL 28

*Remember your word
to your servant, for you
have given me hope.
Psalm 119:49*

Whatever your special need may be, you will find some promise in the Bible suited to it. Do you feel weary because your life is so difficult? Here is the promise: "He gives strength to the weary and increases the power of the weak." Whatever your fears or wants, go to the bank of faith with your Father's handwritten check and say, "Remember your word to your servant, for you have given me hope."

APRIL 29

*You are my refuge
in the day of disaster.
Jeremiah 17:17*

No Christian enjoys constant prosperity. Perhaps the Lord gave you a smooth, bright path at first because you were weak and timid. But now that you are stronger in your spiritual life, you must encounter the riper, rougher experience of God's full-grown children. We need "disasters" to excercise our faith, to prune away the rotten branch of self-dependence and root us more firmly in Christ.

APRIL 30

All the Israelites grumbled.
Numbers 14:2

There are grumblers among Christians now, just as there were in Israel's camp. There are those who cry out when God's rod of discipline falls on them. They ask, "Why am I being tormented like this? What have I done to be disciplined in this way?" Certainly it should help you to deal with the chastening if you recognize your Father's hand in it, "because the Lord disciplines those he loves, and he punishes everyone he accepts as a son".

MAY

MAY 1

*His cheeks are as a bed
of spices, as sweet flowers.
Song of Songs 5:13 KJV*

If I cannot see his whole face, at least let me see his cheeks, for even this glimpse of him refreshes my spirit and yields a variety of delights. In Jesus I find not only one flower, but a whole garden. He is my rose and lily. Precious Lord Jesus, let me know the blessedness that comes from abiding in unbroken fellowship with you.

MAY 2

My prayer is not that you take them out of the world but that you protect them from the evil one.
John 17:15

Here we read of Christ praying that his people would *eventually* be with him, but he does not ask that they be taken from the earth right away. He wants them to stay here. Jesus does not plead for our instant removal by death, because our life on earth is important for others, if not for ourselves. Let your desire be to glorify God by your life *here*, as long as he pleases.

MAY 3

In this world you will have trouble.
John 16:33

Do you wonder why this is? Look *upward* to your heavenly Father and see how pure and holy he is. Do you know that one day you will be like him? Do you think that will happen easily? Won't it take a great deal of refining in the furnace of affliction to purify you? You should expect trouble, then. But don't despair, God is with you to help and strengthen you.

MAY 4

Do men make their own gods?
Yes, but they are not gods!
Jeremiah 16:20

One of the great besetting sins of Israel was idolatry, and the church – the spiritual Israel – is tempted in the same way. Mammon still puts up his golden calf. Self in various forms struggles to make believers slaves, and the flesh sets up altars wherever it can find space. We are committing two evils, forsaking the living God, and turning to idols. May the Lord purge us all from the worship of our modern idols.

MAY 5

*I will be their God, And
they will be my people.
2 Corinthians 6:16*

Can you look up to heaven and say, "My Lord and my God, you are mine because of the *relationship* you have established, entitling me to call you my Father; and you are mine by that holy *fellowship* we have when you reveal yourself to me and I delight in your presence?" If you can, then God says of you, and others like you, "My people." For if God is your God, then the Lord loves you in a special way.

MAY 6

We live in him.
1 John 4:13

Do you want a house for your soul? You may ask, "What is the purchase price?" It is less than proud human nature would like to pay. It is without money, without price. Will you take it on these terms? An eternal lease, nothing to pay, just the upkeep of loving and serving him? Will you take Jesus and "live in him"? When this world melts like a dream, this house will live, sturdier than granite, for it is God himself.

MAY 7

*Many followed him, and
he healed all their sick.
Matthew 12:15*

In every corner of the field, he was triumphant over evil and received the acclaim of delivered captives. He came, he saw, and he conquered everywhere. Whatever my own case may be, the beloved Physician can heal me. Whatever may be the state of the others I am praying for, I have hope in Jesus that he will be able to heal them of their sins. However severe my struggle with sins and sicknesses, I can still rejoice.

MAY 8

The man who was healed had no idea who it was.
John 5:13

Years are short to the happy and healthy, but thirty-eight years of disease must have dragged, seeming long and slow, for this disabled man. This man was *tantalized by the Pharisees* and was unable to cope with them. But this man found a cure for his ignorance: He was *visited by the Lord*, and later he was *found testifying* that "it was Jesus who had made him well" (v. 15).

MAY 9

Who has blessed us ... with every spiritual blessing in Christ.
Ephesians 1:3

In the mysterious ages of the past, the Lord Jesus was chosen by his Father; and we have a share in this choosing, because "he chose us in him before the creation of the world" (Ephesians 1:4). We also have the blessings that come from perfect obedience, finished atonement, resurrection, ascension, and intercession. On his breastplate he wears our names. In his pleas before his Father's throne, he remembers our needs.

MAY 10

But Christ has indeed been raised from the dead.
1 Corinthians 15:20

The whole system of Christianity rests on the fact that Christ has been raised from the dead. For, "if Christ has not been raised, your faith is futile; you are still in your sins". *Our ultimate resurrection* rests here, for, "if the Spirit of him who raised Jesus from the dead is living in you, he who raised Christ from the dead will also give life to your mortal bodies through his Spirit, who lives in you".

MAY 11

I am with you always.
Matthew 28:20

There is Someone who is always the same and always with us. Set your heart on the One who is always faithful to you. Do not build your house on the shifting quicksand of a deceitful world, but found your hopes upon this Rock, which stands firm despite pounding rain and roaring floods. Entrust all your concerns to him who can never be taken from you, who will never leave you, and who will never let you leave him.

MAY 12

*I ... will love him and
show myself to him.
John 14:21*

The Lord Jesus gives special revelations of himself to his people. Such manifestations of Christ have a holy influence on the believer's heart. One effect is *humility*. Another effect is *happiness*. In God's presence there are eternal pleasures. *Holiness* is sure to follow. So we see three results of being near to Jesus – humility, happiness, and holiness. May God give them to you!

MAY 13

*Weeping may remain for
a night, but rejoicing
comes in the morning.
Psalm 30:5*

So let us move on boldly. Even if the night is darker than it has ever been, the morning is coming. That's more than they can say in the darkness of hell. Do you know how to anticipate the joys of heaven, to live in expectation? It is a comforting hope. It may be dark now, but the morning brings light. Our weeping will turn to rejoicing.

MAY 14

*Heirs of God and
co-heirs with Christ.
Romans 8:17*

The unlimited realms of the Father's universe belong to Christ. As God's Son, he is the heir to this fortune, the sole proprietor of the vast creation. He has allowed us to claim the whole estate as ours, too, since we have officially been named as "co-heirs" with him. Why settle for jealousy, selfishness, and greed – which never share their wealth anyway – when Christ is longing for you to join in his happiness?

MAY 15

Everyone who believes is justified.
Acts 13:39

A person who believes in Christ receives a *present* justification. Faith produces this fruit *now*, not at some distant time. Justification is given to the soul at the moment when it accepts Christ as its all in all. *Now* we are pardoned. *Now* our sins are put away. *Now* we stand accepted before God, as if we had never been guilty. "Therefore, there is *now* no condemnation for those who are in Christ Jesus."

MAY 16

God ... richly provides us with everything for our enjoyment.
1 Timothy 6:17

Our Lord Jesus is always giving to us. As long as there is a vessel of grace that is not yet full to the brim, he will not stop pouring the oil of his blessing. He is an ever-shining sun. He is manna that is constantly falling around the camp. He is a rock in the desert, always sending out streams of life. The rain of his grace is always pouring down; the river of his blessing flows on and on; and the wellspring of his love overflows endlessly.

MAY 17

Whoever claims to live in him must walk as Jesus did.
1 John 2:6

Why should Christians imitate Christ? They should do it *for their own sakes*. If they want their souls to be healthy, if they want to avoid the sickness of sin and enjoy the vigor of growing grace, they should let Jesus be their model. But especially, *for Christ's own sake*, follow his example. Do you love your Savior? Is his name precious to you? Be a letter from Christ that is "known and read by everybody".

MAY 18

For in Christ all the fullness of the Deity lives in bodily form, and you have been given fullness in Christ.
Colossians 2:9-10

All of Christ, in his adorable character as the Son of God, is granted to us for our enjoyment. His wisdom directs us, his knowledge instructs us, his power protects us, his justice upholds us, and his love comforts us. He holds nothing back. "All, all, all are yours," he says. "Be satisfied with my grace and be full of my goodness."

MAY 19

I have seen slaves on horseback, while princes go on foot like slaves.
Ecclesiastes 10:7

We must not let our passions and carnal appetites ride in triumph, while our nobler instincts walk in the dust. Grace must reign in our lives as a prince, making the members of our bodies its servants. We were not created to allow our passions to rule over us, but so that we, as kings, might reign with Christ over our spirits, souls, and bodies, to the glory of God the Father.

MAY 20

*Show the wonder
of your great love.
Psalm 17:7*

When we give our offerings, do we also give our hearts? We often fail in this respect, but the Lord never does. His favors always come to us with the love of his heart. He does not send us the leftovers and crumbs from his dining table, but he dips our morsel in his own dish and seasons our meals with the spices of his fragrant affection.

MAY 21

*If ... ye have tasted that
the Lord is gracious.
1 Peter 2:3 KJV*

While this should be a matter of earnest and prayerful inquiry, no one ought to be content as long as there is an "if" about his having tasted that the Lord is gracious. Do not rest, believer, until you have a full assurance of where you stand with Jesus. Do not let anything satisfy you, until, as the Holy Spirit bears witness with your spirit, you are convinced that you are a child of God. Don't be satisfied with *perhaps* or *if* or *maybe*.

MAY 22

He led them by a straight way.
Psalm 107:7

Experiencing great changes, the anxious believer might sometimes ask, "Why am I going through this? Is this part of God's plan for me? Is this any way for God to bring me toward heaven?" Yes, it is. "We must go through many hardships to enter the kingdom of God" (Acts 14:22). So learn to "consider it pure joy" (James 1:2).

MAY 23

*The Lord will fulfill
his purpose for me.
Psalm 138:8*

Clearly, the confidence the psalmist was expressing here was a *divine confidence*. He did not say, "*I* have grace enough to fulfill God's purposes for me. *My* faith is so steady that it will never stagger." No, his dependence was on the Lord alone. He rested on nothing short of the *Lord's* work. It is the Lord who has begun a good work in us, and he has carried it on. But thanks be to God, he will fulfill his purposes for us.

MAY 24

*Praise be to God, who has
not rejected my prayer.
Psalm 66:20*

If we honestly looked at the character of our prayers, we would be surprised that God ever answers them. Some may think that their prayers are worthy of acceptance – like the Pharisees. But the true Christian looks more humbly at his prayers, and if he could retrace his steps, would want to learn how to pray more earnestly. "Pray in the Spirit on all occasions, with all kinds of prayers and requests" (Ephesians 6:18).

MAY 25

O Lord, do not forsake me.
Psalm 38:21

We often pray that God will not forsake us in our times of trial and temptation, but we forget that we need to pray like this *at all times*. "Lord, I am weak. With you, I am strong. Do not forsake me, for my path is dangerous. I cannot do without your guidance. As the hen will not forsake her brood, so cover me forever with your feathers, let me find refuge under your wings."

MAY 26

Cast your cares on the Lord and he will sustain you.
Psalm 55:22

Care can be sinful – even when we are caring about legitimate things – if it is carried to extremes. Our Savior regularly taught that we should avoid anxious concern. Anxiety makes us doubt God's loving-kindness, and so our love for him grows cold. But if, through simple faith in his promise, we cast each burden upon him, we will remain close to him, strengthened against temptation.

MAY 27

And Mephibosheth lived in Jerusalem, because he always ate at the king's table, and he was crippled in both feet.
2 Samuel 9:13

Like Mephibosheth, we may cry unto the King of Glory, "What is your servant, that you should notice a dead dog like me?" But still the Lord blesses us with his friendship, because he sees in us the righteousness of his dearly beloved Jesus. This is the kind of love the Father has for his only begotten Son, that for his sake he raises his lowly brothers from poverty and banishment.

MAY 28

Those he justified,
he also glorified.
Romans 8:30

Here is a precious truth for you, believer. You may be poor or suffering, but it may encourage you to review your "calling" and the consequences that flow from it. As surely as you are God's child, your trials will soon end, and you will bask in his riches. Wait a while, and your weary head will wear a crown of glory, your laboring hand will grab the palm branch of victory.

MAY 29

You ... hate wickedness.
Psalm 45:7

There can hardly be any goodness in a person if he does not hate wickedness. Wickedness dresses up in fine clothes and imitates the language of holiness. But the teachings of Jesus, like his famous whip of small cords, chase it out of the temple – and will not tolerate it in the church. As warm as his love is toward sinners, so hot is his hatred for sin.

MAY 30

Catch for us the foxes, the little foxes that ruin the vineyards.
Song of Songs 2:15

A little thorn may cause much suffering. A little cloud may hide the sun. Little foxes ruin the vineyards. And little sins do mischief to the tender heart. So think about it. What has driven Christ away from you? If you want to live with Christ, watch out for "the little foxes that ruin the vineyards".

MAY 31

*The king also crossed
the Kidron Valley.
2 Samuel 15:23*

It should comfort us to know that Jesus has been tempted in every way that we are. What is our Kidron this morning? Is it a treacherous friend, a sad bereavement, a slanderous attack, a dark sense of foreboding? The King has crossed each of these Kidrons before us. We must banish once and for all the idea that our afflictions are unique, because Jesus has been through it all.

JUNE

JUNE 1

And there was evening, and there was morning – the first day.
Genesis 1:5

Was it true even from the beginning? Did light and darkness divide the realm of time in the first day? Then it is little wonder that my life also changes between the sunshine of prosperity and the midnight of adversity. There will not always be the blaze of noon in my soul. At times I must expect to mourn the loss of previous joys and to seek my Beloved in the night.

JUNE 2

*For the sinful nature desires
what is contrary to the Spirit,
and the Spirit what is contrary
to the sinful nature.
Galatians 5:17*

In every believer's heart there is a constant struggle between the old nature and the new. Are you fighting with the enemy today? Have Satan, the world, and your sinful nature all lined up against you? So do not be afraid. Who can defeat the All-powerful One? You will overcome. Keep fighting, "looking unto Jesus".

JUNE 3

These were potters, and those that dwelt among plants and hedges: there they dwelt with the king for his work.
1 Chronicles 4:23 KJV

We, too, may be engaged in the most menial part of the Lord's work, but it is a great privilege to do anything for "the king". You unknown workers who are busy for your Lord in the middle of the dirt and misery of the lowest of the low, rejoice! Stay close to the king in whatever work you do, and when he writes his chronicles, your name will be recorded.

JUNE 4

*The kindness and love
of God our Savior.
Titus 3:4*

When we meditate on this amazing love, we may even faint with joy. To consider that great Benefactor of the church endowing her with all his wealth – who can comprehend such weighty love? The Holy Spirit sometimes gives us a partial sense of the magnitude of divine love, but our souls even have a hard time containing that! How staggering it would be to see its fullness!

JUNE 5

Then the Lord shut him in.
Genesis 7:16

Outside the ark, it was all ruined, but inside there was rest and peace. Without Christ, we perish. But in Christ Jesus there is perfect safety. Noah was shut in so that he could not even desire to come out. So those who are in Christ Jesus are in him forever. Eternal faithfulness has shut them in, and no amount of devilish malice can drag them out.

JUNE 6

I am unworthy.
Job 40:4

This is actually a comforting thought for the humble sinner. You may think that you cannot approach God because you are so unworthy, but there is not a saint on earth who has not felt unworthy. If Job and Isaiah and Paul were all obliged to say they were unworthy, will you be ashamed to join in the same confession?

JUNE 7

*Let those who love
the Lord hate evil.
Psalm 97:10*

If you truly love your Savior and want to honor him, then "hate evil". How? There is no better cure for the love of evil in a Christian than intimate fellowship with the Lord Jesus. Live close to him, and it will be impossible for you to be at peace with sin.

JUNE 8

*Many others fell slain,
because the battle was God's.
1 Chronicles 5:22*

Friends, as we fight against sin, in our lives and in society, against errors both doctrinal and practical, against spiritual wickedness in high places and low, we are waging God's battle! We need not fear defeat. Attack with the two-edged sword of the Spirit, and you will prevail. With steadfast feet, a strong hand, a fearless heart, and flaming zeal, rush into battle, and the hosts of evil will fly like chaff in the wind.

JUNE 9

The Lord has done great things for us, and we are filled with joy.
Psalm 126:3

Some Christians are sadly prone to look on the dark side of everything. They dwell more on what they have gone through than on what God has done for them. But a Christian whose soul is in a healthy state will come forward joyously and say, "Let me tell you what the Lord has done in my life." "The Lord has done great things for us, and we are filled with joy."

JUNE 10

We live to the Lord.
Romans 14:8

If God wanted it, each of us might have entered heaven at the moment of our conversion. Why then are we still here? Would God keep his children out of paradise for a single moment longer than was necessary? The answer is: We are here so that we may "live to the Lord" and bring others to know his love. We are here to glorify Christ in our daily lives. We are here as workers for him, and as workers together with him.

JUNE 11

We love because he first loved us.
1 John 4:19

But even after God's love is born in our hearts, it must be nourished by him. Love is an exotic plant; it does not grow naturally in human soil. It must be specially watered from above. Love for Jesus is a flower of a delicate nature. Love must feed on love. The very soul and life of our love for God is his love for us.

JUNE 12

*You have been weighed on the
scales and found wanting.
Daniel 5:27*

We should frequently weigh ourselves on the scale of God's Word. If we read God's Word in this way as a test of our spiritual condition, we may stop every so often and say, "Lord, I feel that I haven't yet been here. Bring me here! Give me true repentance, real faith, warmer zeal, more fervent love – as I read about here. Make me more like Jesus. I don't want to be 'found wanting' anymore."

JUNE 13

And whoever wishes, let him take the free gift of the water of life.
Revelation 22:17

Jesus says, "Take freely." He wants no payment. He seeks no special favors. If you are willing, you are invited. So come! How many are there who are rich in their own good works and therefore will not come to Christ? "I refuse to be saved," they say, "in the same way as prostitutes and garbage collectors." Such proud boasters may remain without the living water, but "whoever wishes, let him take the free gift of the water of life".

JUNE 14

Delight yourself in the Lord.
Psalm 37:4

The believer's life is described here as a *delight* in God, so we are reminded that true religion overflows with happiness and joy. The thought of delight in religion is so strange to most people that they probably can't think of two words that are further apart in meaning than *holiness* and *delight*. But believers who know Christ understand that delight and faith are united. Nothing can separate the two.

JUNE 15

Sarah said, "God brought me laughter, and everyone who hears about this will laugh with me."
Genesis 21:6

The Lord Jesus is a deep sea of joy. My soul will dive into it and will be swallowed up in the delights of his companionship. Sarah looked on her Isaac and laughed with her overwhelming emotion, and all her friends laughed with her. When my soul looks at Jesus, I want heaven and earth to unite in joy unspeakable.

JUNE 16

*I give them eternal life,
and they shall never perish.
John 10:28*

Christ himself said, "I give them eternal life, and they shall never perish; no one can snatch them out of my hand" (John 10:28). If his love could fail, these promises would be false. All the doctrines of God's grace would be disproved if one child of God perished. Banish those doubting fears that dishonor God. Get up, shake off the dust, and put on your beautiful garments of faith. Let the eternal life within you express itself in constant rejoicing.

JUNE 17

Help, Lord.
Psalm 12:1

This prayer itself is remarkable, for it is *short*, but *seasonable*. It expresses the deep *sentiments* of the psalmist, and it *suggests* that the Lord is strong enough to help. The answer to this prayer is certain, if the prayer is sincerely offered through Jesus. The Lord has promised that he will not leave his people. He guarantees his aid: "Do not fear, I will help you" (Isaiah 41:13).

JUNE 18

Your redeemer.
Isaiah 54:5

Jesus, our Redeemer, is thoroughly ours – and he is ours forever. All the offices of Christ are held on our behalf. He is King for us, Priest for us, and Prophet for us. But his humanity is also ours, in all its perfection. Our gracious Lord offers to us the spotless virtue of his stainless character. And the superhuman meekness of his death is our boast and glory.

JUNE 19

All of them were filled with the Holy Spirit.
Acts 2:4

The blessings of this day were rich. It is impossible to estimate the full consequences of this sacred filling of the soul. Life, comfort, light, purity, power, peace, and many other precious blessings – all these go along with the Spirit's presence. As the wind, he breathes life into people, blowing where he wants to, animating and sustaining all creation. My we feel his presence today and every day.

JUNE 20

For I will give the command, and I will shake the house of Israel among all the nations as grain is shaken in a sieve, and not a pebble will reach the ground.
Amos 9:9

If you feel like grain on the Lord's floor that has been sifted again and again, take comfort from the fact that the Lord is ultimately in charge of the sieve. He is using it for his glory and for your eternal profit.

JUNE 21

You are the most excellent of men.
Psalm 45:2

O Jesus! Your power, your grace, your justice, your tenderness, your truth, your majesty, and your immutability combine to make up such a man – or rather such a "God-man" – that neither heaven nor earth have seen elsewhere. Your fragrance is a holy scent that the best perfumer could never match. Each spice is fragrant, but the compound is divine.

JUNE 22

*It is he who will build the
temple of the Lord, and he
will be clothed with majesty.
Zechariah 6:13*

There are also the rough stones still in the quarry. These must be cut out and squared. All of this is Christ's own work. Each individual believer is being prepared and polished, made ready for his place in the temple. Afflictions themselves cannot sanctify us – only when they are used by Christ to do so.

JUNE 23

*Ephraim is a flat cake
not turned over.
Hosea 7:8*

The saint in public is a devil in private. He deals in flour by day and in soot by night. The cake is burnt on one side and doughy on the other. If this is the way I am, Lord, please turn me! Turn my unsanctified nature to the fire of your love. Let it feel the sacred glow and let my burnt side cool a little while I learn my own weakness.

JUNE 24

A woman in the crowd called out, "Blessed is the mother who gave you birth and nursed you." He replied, "Blessed rather are those who hear the word of God and obey it."
Luke 11:27-28

So you don't need to cry out, "Blessed is the woman who bore you!" Instead, you can bless the Lord for giving you the privilege of hearing his Word and obeying it. That gives us just as close a relationship with Jesus and just as thorough a knowledge as Mary would have had.

JUNE 25

Go up on a high mountain.
Isaiah 40:9

Now the Christian life is of the same order. When we first believe in Christ, we only see a bit of him. The higher we climb, the more we discover of his beauties. The gray-haired Paul, shivering in a dungeon in Rome, could say, "I know whom I have believed" (2 Timothy 1:12).

JUNE 26

You have become like us.
Isaiah 14:10

Consider the tragedy of the person who professes Christianity but doesn't truly believe. Look deeply at your situation. Are you in Christ? It is the easiest thing in the world to give a lenient verdict when you are putting yourself on trial. But be fair and true here. If your house is not built on the rock, it will fall, and its fall will be great. May the Lord give you sincerity, consistency, and firm commitment.

JUNE 27

But you must not go very far.
Exodus 8:28

The ideas of "dying to the world" and "being buried with Christ" seem ridiculous to carnal minds. Worldly wisdom speaks of "moderation". According to this principle, purity may be desirable, but let's not get too precise about it. Of course, they say, truth should be followed, but one should never denounce error too severely. "Therefore come out from them and be separate" (2 Corinthians 6:17).

JUNE 28

Let us fix our eyes on Jesus.
Hebrews 12:2

The Holy Spirit is always working to turn our eyes from ourselves to Jesus. But Satan's work is just the opposite: he is always trying to get us to think of ourselves instead of Christ. So don't look at your own hand trying to grasp Christ. Look to Christ. Don't look to your own hope, but to Jesus, the source of your hope. Don't look at your faith, but to Jesus, the "author and perfecter of our faith" (Hebrews 12:2).

JUNE 29

God will bring with Jesus those who have fallen asleep in him.
1 Thessalonians 4:14

The idea connected with sleep is "rest", and that is the idea the Spirit wants to convey to us. Sleep makes each night a Sabbath for the day. Sleep shuts the door of the soul and keeps all visitors out for a while, so that the inner life may enjoy its garden of ease.

JUNE 30

*I have given them the
glory that you gave me.
John 17:22*

How great is the generosity of Jesus! He has given us his all. Even if he only donated a tenth of his possessions to our cause, it would make us rich beyond belief. But he was not content until he had given everything. If he had merely allowed us to eat the crumbs of blessing that fell from the table of his mercy, that would be amazing grace. But he will do nothing by halves. He invites us to sit with him and share the feast.

JULY

JULY 1

*On that day living water will flow
... in summer and in winter.
Zechariah 14:8*

The streams of living water that flow from Jerusalem are not dried up by the parching heat of the sultry summer, nor are they frozen by the blustery winds of winter. The seasons change – and you change – but your Lord is always the same. The streams of his love are as deep, as broad, as full as ever. Why would we want to wander to any other stream?

JULY 2

In him our hearts rejoice.
Psalm 33:21

Christians can rejoice even in the deepest distress. Though trouble may surround them, they still sing. The believer is not afraid to die. No, he is even willing to depart. He has seen Jesus as the morning star, and he longs to gaze upon him as the sun in all his strength. Truly, the presence of Jesus is all the heaven we desire.

JULY 3

*And the cows that were
ugly and gaunt ate up the
seven sleek, fat cows.
Genesis 41:4*

Pharaoh's dream has too often been my waking experience. I need to beware of "ugly and gaunt" prayers, praises, duties, and experiences. If I neglect prayer for even a short time, I lose all the spirituality I had attained. If I journey every day toward the goal of my desires, I will reach it. O Lord, may I be nourished in your house, so that I may praise your name.

JULY 4

Sanctify them by the truth.
John 17:17

Sanctification begins in regeneration. The Spirit of God infuses into a person the new living principle that makes him a "new creation" (2 Corinthians 5:17) in Christ Jesus. But there is another factor involved. "Sanctify them," Jesus prayed, "by the *truth*; your word is truth." Hold tightly to the truth; in this way you will be sanctified by the Spirit of God.

JULY 5

Called to be saints.
Romans 1:7

We tend to regard the apostles as if they were "saints" in some special way. Each person whom God has called by his grace and sanctified by his Spirit is a saint. Do not look on the ancient saints as being exempt from weakness. They lived *with* Jesus, they lived *for* Jesus, and so they grew to be *like* Jesus. Let us live by the same Spirit as they did and our sainthood will soon be apparent.

JULY 6

*Whoever listens to me will
live in safety and be at ease,
without fear of harm.
Proverbs 1:33*

When the Israelites provoked God by their continued idolatry, he punished them by withholding both dew and rain, but he also took care of his chosen ones. If God does not save his people *under* heaven, he will save them *in* heaven. You can laugh at the bleakest prospects for the future, for they cannot hurt you.

JULY 7

Brothers, pray for us.
1 Thessalonians 5:25

Allow me this morning to repeat the apostle's request. Pray for us. Pray for all Christian ministers. We will be miserable if your prayers are not backing us up. But we will be very happy if you are supporting us. Pray then that we may be the "earthen vessels" (2Corinthians 4:7 KJV) into which God may put the treasure of his gospel.

JULY 8

*Tell me the secret of
your great strength.
Judges 16:6*

What is the secret of the strength of faith? It rests in the food it feeds on. First, faith considers *what the promise is*. Then faith asks, "*Who gave this promise?*" It is God, God all-powerful, God unchanging. Third, faith remembers *why the promise was given* – namely, for God's glory. Then faith considers the amazing *work of Christ* as being a clear proof of the Father's intention to fulfill his Word.

JULY 9

Forget not all his benefits.
Psalm 103:2

Have you had any deliverances? Have you passed through any rivers, supported by God's presence? Have you walked through any fires unharmed? Have you had any moments when God has uniquely revealed his nature to you? Have you had any special blessings? Let us take the pure gold of thankfulness and the jewels of praise and make them into another crown for Jesus' head.

JULY 10

Fellow citizens with God's people.
Ephesians 2:19

What does it mean to be a citizen of heaven? It means that *we are under heaven's government.* Christ the king of heaven reigns in our hearts. *We share heaven's honors.* For we have joined the assembly of those whose names are written in heaven. As citizens, *we have rights to all the property of heaven.* Its pearly gates and chrysolite walls belong to us. *We enjoy its delights.* In heaven they rejoice over sinners who repent, and so do we.

JULY 11

Christ, after you have suffered a little while, will himself restore you and make you strong, firm and steadfast.
1 Peter 5:10

Every good quality you possess should be an enduring quality. May you be rooted and grounded in love (Ephesians 3:17). May your convictions be deep, your love real, and your desires earnest. May your whole life be firm and steadfast. The Christian is made strong and firmly rooted by all the trials and storms of life.

JULY 12

Sanctified by God the Father.
Jude 1 KJV
Sanctified in Christ Jesus.
1 Corinthians 1:2
Through the sanctifying
work of the Spirit.
1 Peter 1:2

Note the unity of the Three Divine Persons in their gracious acts. In deeds of grace, none of the Persons of the Trinity acts apart from the rest. It is correct to speak of sanctification as the work of the Father, of the Son, and of the Spirit.

JULY 13

But God said to Jonah, "Do you have a right to be angry?"
Jonah 4:9

Anger is not necessarily sinful, but it has such a tendency to run wild. This question may help us: "Do you have a right to be angry?" Does such anger speak well of our Christian faith? Does it glorify God? We must be conquerors of all things through Christ – even our tempers. Our natural tendencies are no excuse for sin. We must ask the Lord to crucify our tempers and renew us in gentleness and meekness, after his own image.

JULY 14

*If you make an altar of
stones for me ... you will defile
it if you use a tool on it.
Exodus 20:25*

God's altar was to be built of unhewn stones, so that no trace of human skill or labor would be seen on it. We trust in our own ability to approach God. But this is all just an effort to take human tools to God's altar. The Lord alone must be exalted in our atonement, and not a single mark of human chisels or hammers will be allowed. Let the Lord Jesus be your altar of atonement and rest in him alone.

JULY 15

The fire must be kept burning on the altar continuously; it must not go out.
Leviticus 6:13

Keep the altar of *private prayer* burning. This is the lifeline of holiness. Are we lukewarm in our private devotions? Is the fire burning dimly in our hearts? Let us give to God our hearts. Let us ask him to keep the fire burning. We should be spending time alone with Jesus.

JULY 16

Each morning everyone gathered as much as he needed.
Exodus 16:21

Try to maintain a sense of your entire dependence on the Lord for the things you enjoy each day. All your comforts lie in his hand. Our Lord wants us to feel this hourly dependence on him. For instance, he asks us to pray for our "daily bread", and promises, "Your strength will equal your days" (Deuteronomy 33:25).

JULY 17

For we know, brothers loved by God, that he has chosen you.
1 Thessalonians 1:4

Many people want to know, even before they look to Christ, whether they are chosen. Look to Jesus and believe on him. Then you will know you are chosen. The assurance of the Holy Spirit will be given to you. Christ was at the everlasting council. He can tell you whether you were chosen or not. Go put your trust in him. There will be no doubt about his having chosen *you*, when you have chosen *him*.

JULY 18

*They will set out last,
under their standards.
Numbers 2:31*

The tribe of Dan brought up the rear when the armies of Israel were on the march. But what did their position matter, since they were as much a part of the nation as the tribes that went first? So cheer up, if you feel that you are last and least. It is a privilege merely to be in this army. Someone must do the menial work for Jesus. Work on and carry your standards high.

JULY 19

The Lord our God has shown us his glory.
Deuteronomy 5:24

God's great design in all his works is the manifestation of his own glory. But how can his glory be revealed to fallen human beings? Our "self" must stand out of the way, so that we may have room to exalt God. This is why he often brings his people into difficult times. When we become aware of our own weakness, we are more prepared to see God's majesty as he comes to deliver us. Trials allow you to experience God's greatness and mercy.

JULY 20

*A deposit guaranteeing
our inheritance.
Ephesians 1:14*

What a delightful thing it is to feed on Jesus! Our experience of Jesus is only a taste of the goodness he has. We have enjoyed the first fruits of the Spirit, and these have made us hunger and thirst for the fullness of the heavenly crop. *Here* we see the manna falling in small bits, but *there* we will eat of the bread of heaven. Anticipate heaven, my friend. You will share in the triumph of his glory.

JULY 21

The daughter of Jerusalem tosses her head as you flee.
Isaiah 37:22

Reassured by the word of the Lord, the poor trembling citizens of Jerusalem grew bold, shaking their heads at Sennacherib's boastful threats. Strong faith enables the servants of God to look with calm contempt on their most haughty foes. *We know that our enemies* seek to destroy our eternal life. *We know that the Most High God is with us.* So put away your fears. The kingdom is safe in the King's hands.

JULY 22

I am your husband.
Jeremiah 3:14

Christ Jesus is joined to his people in a holy marriage. He married his church when she was a chaste virgin, long before she fell under the yoke of slavery. The love of even the best husband on earth is but a faint picture of the flame that burns in Jesus' heart. His mystical union with the church surpasses any human marriage, for he has left his Father, cleaves to his church, and has become one flesh with her.

JULY 23

You were like one of them.
Obadiah 1:11

Edom, the nation descended from Esau, owed Israel some brotherly kindness in times of need. But instead, Edom allied herself with Israel's enemies. Have *you* been "like one of them"? At a party, someone starts telling offensive jokes, and everybody laughs, including you – you are like one of them. Be honest with your own soul. Make sure you are a new creature in Christ Jesus. Side with the afflicted people of God and not with the world.

JULY 24

*Stand firm and you will
see the deliverance the Lord
will bring you today.
Exodus 14:13*

These words contain God's command to the believer in trouble. What do you do when you face terrible trials? *Despair* whispers, "Give it all up." But God wants us to maintain a cheerful courage, rejoicing in his love and faithfulness. True faith does not listen to presumption, or despair, or cowardice, or restlessness. It only hears God say, "Stand firm."

JULY 25

*But he left his cloak in her hand
and ran out of the house.
Genesis 39:12*

If you want to be safe from evil acts, hurry away from any opportunity to do them. Today I may be exposed to great danger, so let me have the serpent's wisdom to stay out of it. It is better to lose my cloak than to lose my character. When I resist the devil, he will flee from me, but when I encounter the lusts of the flesh, *I* have to flee, or else they will win over me. O God of holiness, preserve your Josephs.

JULY 26

Make every effort to add to your faith goodness; and to goodness, knowledge.
2 Peter 1:5

If you want to enjoy your faith to the fullest, with the Spirit's help, do what Scripture says: "Make every effort." Make sure you have *goodness*. Study the Scriptures and get *knowledge*. Add to your knowledge *self-control, perseverance, godliness, brotherly kindness* and *love*. When you are adorned with all these jewels, you will be confident of your calling as a Christian.

JULY 27

Very great and precious promises.
2 Peter 1:4

If you want to know how precious God's promises are and to enjoy them in your own heart, meditate often upon them. Try to receive the promises as the very words of God. You don't need to concentrate on how great the promise is – that may stagger you – but on how great the *promiser* is. That will encourage you. If we meditate on the promises and consider the Promiser, we will ultimately experience their sweetness.

JULY 28

I was senseless and ignorant; I was a brute beast before you.
Psalm 73:22

Remember that this is the confession of a man after God's own heart. He has just been describing how he has begrudged the "prosperity of the wicked". Their problem is that they ignore God. But David finds himself doing the same thing. Are we any better than David? Think back to the times you have doubted God. We, too, are senseless and ignorant. But we may also join the psalmist in saying, "You guide me with your counsel."

JULY 29

Yet I am always with you.
Psalm 73:23

"*Yet*," he says. In spite of all the senselessness and ignorance the psalmist had just been confessing, that did not decrease by one atom the fact that he was saved and accepted, enjoying the blessing of being constantly in God's presence. Believer, you may enter into his confession and assurance. Try to say, in the same spirit as the psalmist, "Yet since I belong to Christ, I am always with God."

JULY 30

Then Peter remembered ... and he broke down and wept.
Mark 14:72

Some have suggested that as long as Peter lived, whenever he remembered his denial of Christ, the fountain of his tears began to flow. This is not unlikely, because his sin was very great — even though he was completely forgiven, by God's grace. Many of us who have been redeemed share a similar experience, now that the Spirit has removed our natural hearts of stone.

JULY 31

I in them.
John 17:23

Consider how deep this union is between our souls and the person of Christ. He has set before us an open door. We must not be slow to enter. The Lord Jesus is not far away, he has built a house next door to ours. No, even more, he has moved in with us. Seek the Lord, for he is near. Embrace him; he is your brother. Hold him close to your heart, for he is your own flesh and blood.

AUGUST

AUGUST 1

*Let me go to the fields and
pick up the leftover grain.
Ruth 2:2*

Troubled Christian, come and glean today in the field of promise. There is an abundant supply of precious promises here that will meet your needs. Do you want to pick up some "leftover grain" from the field of Scripture? "Come to me, all you who are weary and burdened, and I will give you rest" (Matthew 11:28). Our Master's field is very rich. Look at all the promises. Gather them up and feed on them with joy.

AUGUST 2

*Who works out everything
in conformity with the
purpose of his will.
Ephesians 1:11*

Since we believe God is all-wise, we must believe he has a plan in his work of salvation. What would creation have been without his design? Is there a fish in the sea, a bird in the air, that was formed by chance? He knows the end from the beginning. He sees where each of us belongs. In the end, it will be clearly seen that God accomplished every part of this great work of grace.

AUGUST 3

The Lamb is its lamp.
Revelation 21:23

Quietly contemplate the Lamb as the light of heaven. Light in Scripture is a symbol of joy. And this is the joy of heaven: *Jesus* chose us, loved us, bought us, cleansed us, robed us, kept us, glorified us. We will be in heaven entirely because of Jesus. Light is also a source of *beauty*. When light is gone, there is no beauty to be seen. Light also symbolizes *knowledge*. In heaven, our knowledge will be perfect. Whatever light there is, Jesus will be at the center and soul of it.

AUGUST 4

*The people who know their
God will firmly resist him.
Daniel 11:32*

Every believer understands that knowing God is the best form of knowledge we can have. It strengthens our *faith*, our *love* and also strengthens *hope*. Knowledge also gives us reasons for *patience*. There is no Christian virtue that is not advanced by the knowledge of God. That makes it crucial that we grow not only in grace, but also in the "knowledge of our Lord and Savior Jesus Christ" (2 Peter 3:18).

AUGUST 5

*And we know that in all
things God works for the
good of those who love him.
Romans 8:28*

There are some things a believer can be absolutely sure about. We know, for instance, that God is in control. We also know that God is always wise. So believing that God is in control, that he governs wisely, and that he brings good out of evil, we can rest assured, able to meet each trial calmly as it comes.

AUGUST 6

Watchman, what of the night?
Isaiah 21:11 KJV

What enemies are out there? Sins creep from their lurking places when it is dark. Our heavenly Protector foresees the attacks that are about to come against us. He prays that our faith will not fail. *What weather is coming* for the church? We need to read the signs of the times. *What stars are visible?* What precious promises apply to our present situation? O Watchman, you who sound the alarm, give us comfort, too.

AUGUST 7

The upright love thee.
Song of Songs 1:4 KJV

Believers love Jesus with a deeper affection than they would dare to give any other being. People have tried to separate the faithful from their Master, but in every age these attempts have been fruitless. Yet we constantly lament the fact that we cannot love *more*. Wouldn't it be wonderful if we could put together all our love, from all believers, in one great collection, and offer it to our great Lord.

AUGUST 8

They ... spin a spider's web.
Isaiah 59:5

The spider's web is a picture of the hypocrite's religion. How? *It is meant to catch his prey.* Reputation, praise, and advancement – these are the flies that hypocrites catch in their webs. A spider's web is *a marvel of skill*. But isn't the hypocrite's religion just as amazing? One final thought: Cobwebs *are not to be tolerated in God's house.* Be sure you're resting on something sturdier.

AUGUST 9

*The city does not need the sun or
the moon to shine on it.
Revelation 21:23*

The inhabitants of that better world have no need of creature comforts, medicine, sleep or teachers. The Lord himself teaches them. What a blessed time that will be, when we will finally surpass every secondary blessing and rest on the bare arm of God! What a glorious day, when we will find our joy each day in God and not in his creatures, in the Lord and not in his works. Our souls will have attained perfect bliss.

AUGUST 10

Christ, who is your life.
Colossians 3:4

Paul's marvelously rich expression indicates that Christ is the *source* of our life. He is also the *substance* of our spiritual life. It is by his life that we live. He is in us, the hope of glory, the spring of our actions, the central thought that moves every other thought. Christ is the *solace* of our life. All our true joys come from him. Christ is the *model* for our life. If we live in close fellowship with Jesus, we will grow to be like him.

AUGUST 11

How I long for the months gone by.
Job 29:2

Many Christians view the past with pleasure, but are dissatisfied with the present. There are many possible causes for such a state. It may arise through a *neglect of prayer*. Or it may be the result of *idolatry*. Their hearts may be preoccupied with something else. Christian, if you are longing for the "months gone by", don't just *wish* for a return to the way it was – go to your Master. Ask for his grace and strength to help you walk more closely with him.

AUGUST 12

*The Lord reigns, let
the earth be glad.
Psalm 97:1*

There is no reason to be sad as long as this wonderful sentence is true. *On earth*, the Lord's power controls the rage of the wicked just as easily as it controls the rage of the sea. *In hell*, the tormented spirits acknowledge God's supremacy. *In heaven* no one doubts the sovereignty of the Eternal King. All fall on their faces to do him homage. May we arrive soon in that city of the great King!

AUGUST 13

*The cedars of Lebanon
that he planted.
Psalm 104:16*

Lebanon's cedars are symbolic of the Christian. *They owe their planting entirely to the Lord.* This is true of every child of God. We are not man planted or self-planted but God planted. Also the cedars of Lebanon *do not rely on man for their watering.* So it is with the Christian who has learned to live by faith. Finally, the majesty of the cedars is *for the glory of God alone.* To him be all the glory.

AUGUST 14

*For you make me glad
by your deeds, O Lord.
Psalm 92:4*

Do you believe that your sins are forgiven, that Christ has fully atoned for them? Then you should be very happy. Along with your gladness, then, be *grateful and loving*. Express your love in strong ways. Since you have been forgiven freely in Christ, go and tell others the joyful news of God's mercy.

AUGUST 15

He went out to the field one evening to meditate.
Genesis 24:63

Isaac chose a good thing to do. If we were wise, we would spend time meditating on God's Word. We would all know more, live closer to God, and grow in grace. Isaac chose a good place to do it. All of creation points to its Maker, so even the fields can be a holy environment. Isaac chose a good time to do it. The glory of the setting sun delights us, and the oncoming night brings awe. The Lord will meet you wherever you are – go to meet him.

AUGUST 16

*Ascribe to the Lord
the glory due his name.
Psalm 29:2*

God's glory is the result of his nature and his actions. He is glorious in his character, for he holds within him everything that is holy, good, and lovely. Glorious actions flow from his character. He is concerned that the glory associated with these actions should be given back to him and to him only. We should take care to *walk humbly before the Lord.* There is room for only one glory receiver in the universe.

AUGUST 17

*Remember, O Lord,
your great mercy.
Psalm 25:6*

Meditate a little on the mercy of the Lord. It is *tender mercy*. With a gentle, loving touch, he heals the heartbroken and binds up their wounds. It is *great mercy*. His mercy is like himself – it is infinite. It is *undeserved mercy*. Deserved mercy is just another name for justice. It is *rich mercy*. It lifts our spirits and soothes our wounds. It is *abounding mercy* – the supply is not exhausted. And it is *unfailing mercy*. It will never leave you.

AUGUST 18

Foreigners have entered the holy places of the Lord's house.
Jeremiah 51:51

This was a shameful thing for the Lord's people. The Holy Place of the temple was reserved for priests alone. We see similar causes for grief nowadays. How many people in our land consider themselves Christians merely because they live here? In how many churches do people take communion without any realization of what it means? We should examine *ourselves* to see if we belong at the Lord's Table.

AUGUST 19

He will stand and shepherd his flock in the strength of the Lord.
Micah 5:4

Christ reigns in his church as a *shepherd-king*. He has supremacy, but it is the superiority of a wise and tender shepherd over his needy and loving flock. His reign is *practical*. He is actively engaged in providing for his people. His reign is *continual*. His reign is *powerful*. Wherever Christ is, there is God. We are fortunate to belong to such a shepherd, whose humanity interacts with us and whose divinity protects us.

AUGUST 20

The sweet psalmist of Israel.
2 Samuel 23:1 KJV

Of all the saints whose lives are recorded in Scripture, David has the most striking, varied, and instructive experiences. In his history, we find trials and temptations we don't come across elsewhere. David knew the trials of all levels of humanity. This may explain why David's psalms are so universally loved by Christians. Whatever our frame of mind, whether ecstasy or depression, David has described our emotions perfectly.

AUGUST 21

He who refreshes others will himself be refreshed.
Proverbs 11:25

This teaches us a great lesson: To get, we must give. To make ourselves happy, we must make others happy. How does this work? First, our efforts to be useful bring out our own powers of usefulness. We often find that, in trying to teach others, we learn a great deal ourselves. Refreshing others also humbles us. We see how God's grace overshadows our efforts. So "give, and it will be given to you".

AUGUST 22

O daughters of Jerusalem, I charge you – if you find my lover, what will you tell him? Tell him I am faint with love.
Song of Songs 5:8

This is the language of the believer who longs for fellowship with Jesus. He is faint with love. Believing souls are never perfectly at ease unless they are close to Christ. Behind this desperation, there is a blessing. Jesus said, "Blessed are those who hunger and thirst for righteousness" (Matthew 5:6).

AUGUST 23

The sound of weeping and of crying will be heard in it no more.
Isaiah 65:19

Why will there be no weeping in heaven? *All external causes of grief will be gone. We will be perfectly sanctified.* No longer will temptations lure us away from the living God. *All fear of change will be past.* We will know that we are eternally secure. *Every desire will be fulfilled.* All our faculties will be completely satisfied.

AUGUST 24

*One who breaks open the
way will go up before them.
Micah 2:13*

Because Jesus has gone before us, everything is different. He has conquered every enemy that stood in our way. So cheer up! Not only has Christ traveled the road before you, but he has also defeated your enemies. Whatever foes might come up against the Christian, they have all been overcome. Through Christ, God has taken away all the power that is wielded against us.

AUGUST 25

His fruit is sweet to my taste.
Song of Songs 2:3

Faith, in Scripture, is spoken of in terms of all the senses. Faith begins with *hearing*. We hear God's Word. Then our minds *look* at the truth. When we appropriate the mercies of Christ, claiming them for our own, that is *touch*. Then comes the enjoyment – peace, delight, communion. This is the *tasting* of faith.

AUGUST 26

He ordained his covenant forever.
Psalm 111:9

The Lord's people delight in the covenant itself. We love to contemplate how *old* the covenant is. Our hearts thrill with joy as we consider how *unchanging* the covenant is. Neither time nor eternity, life nor death, will ever be able to violate it. This covenant is a rich treasure chest, a warehouse overflowing with good food, a fountain of life-giving water, a treaty of lasting peace, and a haven of joy.

AUGUST 27

*How long will they
refuse to believe in me?
Numbers 14:11*

Work as hard as you can to keep the monster of unbelief away. In your case, Christian, it is all the worse. You have received so many mercies from the Lord in the past, how can you doubt him now? Jesus has never given us the slightest grounds for suspicion. He has been consistently affectionate and true to us. So away with this lying traitor, unbelief! He is only trying to cut the ties between us and Christ.

AUGUST 28

Oil for the light.
Exodus 25:6

We all need this oil. Our lamps will not burn long without it. There is no "oil well" within our own natures, so we need to go out and get some. It was not just any oil that was to be used for the tabernacle lamps. The oil of God's true grace is pure and free from dregs. So our light is clear and bright. We should be praying for ourselves, our ministers, and our churches, that we might always have a full supply of the oil of God's grace.

AUGUST 29

Have mercy on me, O God.
Psalm 51:1

Even the most experienced and most honored of Christians can only approach God by his free gift of grace. Those who merely profess their faith may boast of their spirituality, but the true children of God cry for mercy. We need the Lord to have mercy on our good works, our prayers, our preachings, our offerings, all our holiest things. Remember that God's inexhaustible mercy is waiting for us.

AUGUST 30

Wait for the Lord.
Psalm 27:14

Waiting may seem easy, but it takes years to learn. There are times of confusion when the most zealous soul, eagerly wanting to serve the Lord, just does not know what to do. *Wait in prayer.* Call on God and spread the case before him. *Wait with a simple heart, in faith,* and *in quiet patience.* Don't complain about your situation, but thank God for it. Accept it as it is and put it all into God's hands.

AUGUST 31

And wait in hope for my arm.
Isaiah 51:5

In times of severe trial, the Christian has nothing on earth he can trust in, so he is compelled to cast himself on the Lord. Sometimes, however, we find it hard to get to God because we have too many friends. But the poor, friendless man has nowhere else to turn. He flies to his Father's arms and is happily embraced. Do not dishonor your Lord by entertaining doubts and fears. Be strong in your faith, giving glory to God.

SEPTEMBER

SEPTEMBER 1

*You guide me with your
counsel, and afterward you
will take me into glory.
Psalm 73:24*

The psalmist felt his need for divine guidance. He had just been discovering the foolishness of his own heart, and to keep himself from being led astray, he decided to let God's wisdom guide him. We have wandered, strayed, sinned – but he will welcome us home. Live with this assurance in your heart today.

SEPTEMBER 2

Simon's mother-in-law was in bed with a fever, and they told Jesus about her.
Mark 1:30

Peter's house was probably a poor fisherman's hut, but the Lord of Glory entered it, lodged there, and worked a miracle. We can't be sure that the Lord will immediately remove all disease from those we love, yet prayer is more likely to bring about healing than anything else. Where this does not happen, we must meekly bow to the Lord's will. He is the one who determines life and death.

SEPTEMBER 3

You whom I love.
Song of Songs 1:7

Can you truly say this about Jesus – "you whom I love?" Many can only say that they *hope* they love him, or they *think* they love him. But only the shallowest spirituality will stay at this level. True love for Christ always comes from the Holy Spirit. He may bring it about, but the logical reason for loving Jesus lies in Jesus himself. *Why* do we love Jesus? *Because he first loved us* (1 John 4:19). Because he "gave himself up for us" (Ephesians 5:2).

SEPTEMBER 4

"I am willing," he said. "Be clean!"
Mark 1:41

The word of the Lord Jesus has authority. Jesus speaks, and it is done. Leprosy yielded to no human remedies, but it went running the moment it heard the Lord's "Be clean!" The sinner is in a plight worse than the leper. Sinners should follow the leper's example, coming to Christ and begging on their knees, summoning whatever faith they have, to say, "If you are willing, you can make me clean." Jesus heals all who come.

SEPTEMBER 5

*Woe to me that I dwell in
Mesech, that I live among
the tents of Kedar!
Psalm 120:5*

As a Christian, you have to live in the midst of an ungodly world. In Jesus' priestly prayer, he pointedly did *not* ask his Father to take believers out of this troublesome world (John 17:15). Remember that people are watching you. Because you are a Christian, they expect more from you than from others. Let your goodness be the only thing "wrong" with you.

SEPTEMBER 6

In a crooked and depraved generation, in which you shine like stars in the universe.
Philippians 2:15

We use lights *to make things clear*. A Christian's life should shine to such an extent that a person could not live with him for a week without knowing the gospel. Lights are also intended for *guidance*. We should be pointing sinners to the Savior. A Christian ought to be a comforter, with kind words on his lips and sympathy in his heart.

SEPTEMBER 7

Since they could not get him to Jesus because of the crowd, they made an opening in the roof above Jesus and, after digging through it, lowered the mat the paralyzed man was lying on.
Mark 2:4

Faith is full of inventions. The house was full. A crowd blocked the door. But faith found a way of getting to Jesus and bringing the sick man to him. If we cannot get sinners to Jesus by ordinary methods, we must use extraordinary ones.

SEPTEMBER 8

Your fruitfulness comes from me.
Hosea 14:8

How does this happen? Through our *union* with Christ. The fruit on the branch of a tree is connected to the roots of that tree. Sever that connection, and the branch dies – no fruit is produced. Similarly, we bring forth fruit from our union with Christ. Treasure your union with Christ. It is the source of all your fruitfulness. If you weren't joined to Jesus, you would be very barren.

SEPTEMBER 9

I will answer you and tell you great and unsearchable things you do not know.
Jeremiah 33:3

Some parts of the Christian experience are reserved and special. Not all the developments of spiritual life are easy to attain. There are the common feelings of repentance, along with faith, joy, and hope, that are enjoyed by the entire family. But there is an upper realm of communion with Christ which goes beyond where most believers are. Only God can take us there.

SEPTEMBER 10

*Jesus went up on a mountainside
and called to him those he
wanted, and they came to him.
Mark 3:13*

Jesus stands on the mountain, always above the world in terms of holiness, zeal, love, and power. The people he calls must go up the mountain to him. They must seek to rise to his level by living in constant communion with him. This morning, let us climb the mount of communion. There we may be set apart and empowered for our lifework.

SEPTEMBER 11

Be separate.
2 Corinthians 6:17

The Christian is *in* the world but should not be *of* the world. He should be distinct from the world in terms of *his life's goal*. You should also differ from the world in your *spirit*. Waiting humbly before God, always aware of his presence, enjoying close fellowship with him, seeking to know his will – in all these ways you will prove you belong to him. Your *actions* should also set you apart. You must avoid wrong for Christ's sake.

SEPTEMBER 12

The Lord is a jealous ... God.
Nahum 1:2

Your Lord is very jealous of your love. Didn't he choose you? Didn't he buy you with his own blood? He hates it when you insist that you are your own person or that you belong to the world. *He is also very jealous of our company.* We should be talking with Jesus more than anyone else. He wants us to abide in him, to stay close to him. But his jealousy can also comfort us. For if he loves us this much, he will certainly allow nothing to harm us.

SEPTEMBER 13

As they pass through the Valley of Baca, they make it a place of springs; the autumn rains also cover it with pools.
Psalm 84:6

What is the lesson here? When someone finds comfort for himself, the benefits often overflow to others. Grace can be compared to rain – in its purity, its refreshment, its source (in the heavens), and the will of God that sends it. I pray that you may have showers of blessing, that the pools dug by others may overflow for you.

SEPTEMBER 14

*There were also other
boats with him.
Mark 4:36*

Jesus was the Admiral of the sea that night. His presence preserved the whole fleet. It is good to sail with Jesus, even if you are in a little ship. When we sail in Christ's company, we can't be assured of fair weather. Furious storms rage even around our Lord's vessel, so we shouldn't expect the sea not to toss our little boat. When we go with Jesus, we face the same obstacles he does, but we know we will eventually reach land again.

SEPTEMBER 15

He will have no fear of bad news.
Psalm 112:7

Christian, you should not dread the arrival of bad news. If you did not have your God to run to, that would be different. Trust in the Lord. How can you glorify God if you play the coward? If you are doubting and despairing, as if there were no hope, how does that magnify the Lord? Take courage. Rely on the faithfulness of God. "Do not let your heart be troubled" (John 14:1).

SEPTEMBER 16

*You may participate
in the divine nature.
2 Peter 1:4*

What does this mean? To participate in the divine nature is not to become God. That cannot be. The *essence* of deity is not participated in. There will always be a gulf – in terms of essence – between the creature and the Creator. Yet Adam and Eve were made "in the image of God", and we, by the renewal of the Holy Spirit, are *re*made in his image – so even more than the first couple, we participate in God's nature.

SEPTEMBER 17

Bring the boy to me.
Mark 9:19

In despair, the boy's disappointed father turned from the disciples to Jesus. But the child was delivered from the evil one when his father obeyed Jesus' simple command: "Bring the boy to me." Children are a precious gift from God, but a lot of anxiety comes with them. They may be filled with the Spirit of God or possessed by a spirit of evil. In each case, the Word of God gives the simple answer for curing their ills: "Bring them to me."

SEPTEMBER 18

Since we live by the Spirit, let us keep in step with the Spirit.
Galatians 5:25

The two most important things in our religion are the *life of faith* and the *walk of faith*. These are vital points for the Christian. You will never find true faith unaccompanied by true godliness. On the other hand, you will never find a truly holy life that is not rooted in a living faith in Jesus. O Lord, give us faith within, which comes out in holy lives, glorifying you.

SEPTEMBER 19

*It is for freedom that
Christ has set us free.
Galatians 5:1*

We are free. We have free access to the Bible. We are free to enjoy the promises of God. Scripture is a treasury always well stocked with grace. In serious trials, this freedom can comfort and cheer you. You are free to enjoy everything that is stored up for you in Christ – wisdom, righteousness, sanctification, and redemption. What a great freedom this is!

SEPTEMBER 20

The sword of the Lord, and of Gideon.
Judges 7:20 KJV

Gideon ordered his men to do two things. They carried torches, but hid them in earthen pitchers. Their first task was to break the pitchers, at the proper signal, and let the light shine. But they also had trumpets. The second task was to blow the trumpets and shout, " The sword of the Lord, and of Gideon!" This is precisely what all Christians must do. First, *we must shine.* Second, we *must boldly proclaim* Christ crucified for sinners.

SEPTEMBER 21

I will rejoice in doing them good.
Jeremiah 32:41

Why should God take such pleasure in us? Yet that is exactly what he says to poor, fallen creatures like ourselves, corrupted by sin, but saved, exalted, and glorified by his grace. What strong language he uses to express his happiness! We should certainly join his song, singing, "I will rejoice in the Lord, I will be joyful in God my Savior" (Habakkuk 3:18).

SEPTEMBER 22

Let Israel rejoice in their Maker.
Psalm 149:2

You have every reason to be glad, my friend, but make sure your gladness has its source *in the Lord.* You can be glad that the Lord reigns. Rejoice that he sits on the throne. You can sing with the psalmist, "God, my joy and my delight" (Psalm 43:4). Every attribute of God becomes a fresh ray in the sunlight of our gladness. We should never stop singing, for his new mercies each day should inspire new songs of thanksgiving.

SEPTEMBER 23

Accepted in the beloved.
Ephesians 1:6 KJV

What a privilege! You may look at yourself and say, "There is nothing acceptable *here*!" But look at Christ – there is everything acceptable *there*. Your sins bother you. But God has put your sins behind his back and accepted you in the Righteous One. You regularly fight with temptation, but you are accepted in the One who has overcome the powers of evil. Rest assured of your glorious standing in Christ, the beloved.

SEPTEMBER 24

I was ashamed to ask the king for soldiers and horsemen to protect us from enemies on the road, because we had told the king, "The gracious hand of our God is on everyone who looks to him, but his great anger is against all who forsake him."
Ezra 8:22

Since Ezra could not bring himself to trust in human protection, the caravan set out guarded only by God. Unfortunately, few believers today rely on God alone. We must learn to honor God by counting on him first of all.

SEPTEMBER 25

*Just and the one who justifies
those who have faith in Jesus.
Romans 3:26*

Since we have been justified by faith, we have peace with God. Conscience no longer accuses us. Judgment is now in our favor. Christ has paid our debt. God is just. If God is just, as a sinner I must be punished. But Jesus takes the punishment for me. My hope, then, rests not in the fact that I am a sinner, but that I am a sinner for whom Christ died.

SEPTEMBER 26

Among the myrtle trees in a ravine.
Zechariah 1:8

The vision in this chapter describes the condition of Israel in Zechariah's day. But as we look at it, it can describe the church as it exists today in the world. The church is compared to a grove of myrtle trees flourishing in a small valley. It is *hidden*, unobserved, secret. We also find a hint of *tranquil security*. Even when opposed and persecuted, the church has a peace that the world cannot give – and cannot take away.

SEPTEMBER 27

*Blessed are you, O Israel!
Who is like you, a people
saved by the Lord?
Deuteronomy 33:29*

Anyone who says Christianity makes people miserable knows nothing about it. When we become Christians, we enter God's family. And why would God give all the happiness to his enemies and make his own children mourn? Should the sinner, who has no interest in Christ, be rich in joy, while we go moping like beggars? No, you can rejoice in the Lord always, and glory in your inheritance.

SEPTEMBER 28

*From heaven the Lord
looks down and sees all.
Psalm 33:13*

There's probably no image that shows God in a better light than when he is depicted stooping from his throne, coming down from heaven to see firsthand the wants and needs of his people. He regularly bends his ear to hear the prayers of dying sinners who long for reconciliation. He pays special attention to us: don't ever think that God sits high and mighty and doesn't care about you.

SEPTEMBER 29

If the disease has covered his whole body, he shall pronounce that person clean.
Leviticus 13:13

This rule seems strange at first, but there is wisdom in it. If the leper had been completely infected by the disease and still survived, that proved his constitution was basically sound. We, too, are lepers. When someone sees that he is completely lost, ravaged by sin, and pleads guilty before the Lord – then he is clean through the blood of Jesus and the grace of God.

SEPTEMBER 30

*Sing the glory of his name;
make his praise glorious!
Psalm 66:2*

It is not up to us whether or not we praise God. Praise is due to God, and every Christian, as a recipient of his grace, owes him thanks daily. It is not only a pleasurable exercise, but an absolute obligation. Why do you think he has blessed you? So that you may bless him back. If you do not praise God, you are not bringing forth the fruit that he, the Divine Gardener, has a right to expect from you.

OCTOBER

OCTOBER 1

*At our door is every delicacy,
both new and old, that I have
stored up for you, my lover.
Song of Songs 7:13*

The beloved bride wants to give Jesus all she can. Our hearts are filled with "every delicacy, both new and old", stored up for Jesus, the lover of our soul. We have *new* delicacies. We brim with new life, and *old* delicacies – that joy we had when we first came to know the Lord. Whatever blessings or talents or virtues we have, let's give them all to our Beloved.

OCTOBER 2

*The hope that is stored
up for you in heaven.
Colossians 1:5*

Our hope in Christ and the heavenly future he prepares for us keeps us going. It cheers us up to think of heaven, because all that we desire awaits us. Through God's Spirit, the hope of heaven can produce great righteousness within us. The person who has this hope inside has a new vigor in his work – for the joy of the Lord is his strength (Nehemiah 8:10).

OCTOBER 3

Are not all angels ministering spirits sent to serve those who will inherit salvation?
Hebrews 1:14

Angels are the invisible bodyguards of the saints of God. Loyalty to their Lord leads them to take a deep interest in the children he loves. In biblical times, God's people were sometimes visited by angels. This still happens, though we don't see them. The angels of God still ascend and descend to visit the heirs of salvation (Genesis 28:12), only now their ladder is Jesus himself.

OCTOBER 4

*When evening comes,
there will be light.
Zechariah 14:7*

We often dread the onslaught of old age. We forget that, "when evening comes, there will be light". We don't need to dread this time; we can look forward to it. Even pain does not break the calm of this twilight time, for strength is made perfect in weakness (2 Corinthians 12:9).

OCTOBER 5

So he got up and ate and drank. Strengthened by that food, he traveled forty days and forty nights.
1 Kings 19:8

God supplies us with great strength when we need it, but he wants us to use that strength in his service, not in wanton pleasure seeking or boasting. We eat the bread of heaven so that we may be strengthened to serve our Master. Earth should be a preparation for heaven. Heaven is a place where the saints feast and work.

OCTOBER 6

*Whoever drinks the water I
give him will never thirst.
John 4:14*

The one who believes in Jesus finds enough to satisfy him now and forever. The heart is as insatiable as the grave until Jesus enters it. Then it is a cup that overflows. The true saint is so completely satisfied with Jesus that he is no longer thirsty – except for another drink from the living fountain. That is the only kind of thirst you should feel, my friend, not a thirst of pain but of love.

OCTOBER 7

Why have you brought this trouble on your servant?
Numbers 11:11

Why does our heavenly Father bring troubles on his servants? *To try our faith.* If our faith is worth anything, it will stand the test. If you can only trust God when your friends are faithful, your body healthy, and your business profitable, then your faith is poor. True faith relies on the Lord's faithfulness when friends are gone, when the body is sick, when spirits are depressed, and when it seems that even God is hiding his face.

OCTOBER 8

Put out into deep water, and let down the nets for a catch.
Luke 5:4

This story teaches us, first, *the necessity of human effort*. The catch of fishes was miraculous, but it still required the use of the fisherman, his boat, and his net. In the saving of souls, the same principle applies. God uses human means. It is certainly his grace alone that saves people, but he still chooses to use the foolishness of preaching. So let us go about our soul fishing today, looking upward in faith and outward in compassion.

OCTOBER 9

Able to keep you from falling.
Jude 24

In a way, the path to heaven is very safe. But in another sense, it is the most dangerous road you could travel. It is beset with difficulties. One false step and down we go. We also have many enemies trying to push us down. Only an Almighty arm can save us from these invisible foes, who seek to destroy us. We have such an arm enlisted in our defence. He has promised to be faithful. He is more than able to keep us from falling.

OCTOBER 10

*Before his glorious
presence without fault.
Jude 24*

Turn around that wonderful phrase in your mind: "without fault". We are far from that now. How will Jesus make *us* flawless? He will wash us clean from our sins in his own blood, until we are as fair as God's purest angel. Christians will not be out of place in heaven. What a great day that will be! Sin gone, Satan shut out, and temptation out of the way – and we are presented "without fault" before God!

OCTOBER 11

Let us lift up our hearts and our hands to God in heaven.
Lamentations 3:41

The act of prayer teaches us our own unworthiness. This is a very important lesson for proud beings like us. A true prayer is an inventory of wants, a catalog of necessities, that reveals to us our hidden poverty. Through prayer, we stake our claim on divine wealth, but we also confess our human emptiness. Prayer turns human folly into heavenly wisdom and gives to troubled mortals the peace of God.

OCTOBER 12

I meditate on your precepts.
Psalm 119:15

Sometimes solitude is better than company, and silence is wiser than speech. We would be better Christians if we spent more time alone, waiting on God, meditating on his Word, gathering spiritual strength to serve him. Why should we muse upon the things of God? Because they nourish us. Hearing, reading, studying, and learning – all of these require digestion in order to be truly useful, and digesting truth involves meditation.

OCTOBER 13

Godly sorrow brings repentance.
2 Corinthians 7:10

Genuine spiritual mourning for sin is *the work of God's Holy Spirit*. Repentance is too precious a flower to grow naturally. Repentance is always the result of God's supernatural grace. True repentance *always involves Jesus*. We must have one eye on our sin and another on the cross. Better still, we should fix both eyes on Christ and see our sins only in the light of his love.

OCTOBER 14

I consider everything a loss compared to the surpassing greatness of knowing Christ Jesus my Lord.
Philippians 3:8

Our knowledge of Christ is *personal*. I cannot rely on anyone else's relationship with Jesus. I must know him *myself*. It is an *intelligent* knowledge. I know him not as some visionary might dream of him, but as Scripture shows him to be. I must know his human nature as well as his divine nature. Sit at Jesus' feet and get to know him.

OCTOBER 15

*But who can endure the
day of his coming?
Malachi 3:2*

Jesus' first coming was quiet. But even then there were few who passed the test. Those who claimed to be waiting for their Savior showed how shallow their convictions were. But what will his second advent be like? Can any sinner even stand to think of it? What will the day be like when the living Savior summons the living and dead before him? Yet his beloved, blood-washed people look forward with joy to his appearing.

OCTOBER 16

Jesus said to them,
"Come and have breakfast."
John 21:12

With these words this morning, you are invited into a holy *nearness to Jesus*. This invitation also speaks of an even closer *union with Jesus*, because the only food we can feast on when we're with Jesus is Jesus himself. This also welcomes us into *fellowship with the saints*. Even if we cannot all *feel* the same way, we can all *feed* the same way, on the bread of life. Get closer to Jesus.

OCTOBER 17

But David thought to himself, "One of these days I will be destroyed by the hand of Saul." 1 Samuel 27:1

This thought that David had was false. The Lord had never deserted him. Don't we doubt God in the same way? Have we ever had the slightest reason to doubt our Father's goodness? No! Our God has never left us! Lord, throw down the Jezebel of our unbelief, and let the dogs devour it.

OCTOBER 18

*Your carts overflow
with abundance.
Psalm 65:11*

What are these "carts" that overflow with good things for us? One special one is certainly the cart of prayer. If a believer frequents the prayer closet, he or she will never lack spiritual nourishment. But there's another cart that overflows with nourishment for the Christian – the cart of communion. How delightful it is to have fellowship with Jesus! Enjoy his presence, and you will be greatly satisfied.

OCTOBER 19

Mere infants in Christ.
1 Corinthians 3:1

Do you feel that your spiritual life is weak? Does it bother you that your faith is small, your love feeble? Cheer up. You still have reason to be thankful. Remember that in some things you are equal to the most experienced, most full-grown Christian. You are bought with the blood of Christ, just as much as the greatest saint is. You are just as much an adopted child of God. You have just as much right to the promises in the covenant as the most advanced believer has.

OCTOBER 20

In all things grow up into him.
Ephesians 4:15

Many Christians have stunted their growth in spiritual things. There's no advance, no upspringing. They *exist*, but they do not *grow*. Should we be satisfied just believing in Christ – at least we are "safe" – and not longing to move more and more into his fullness? No! As good traders in heaven's market, we should keep trying to gain more of the knowledge of our Lord.

OCTOBER 21

For Christ's love compels us.
2 Corinthians 5:14

How much do you owe the Lord? Has he ever done anything for you? Has he forgiven your sins? Has he written your name in his book of life? Then do something for Jesus that is worthy of his love. How will you feel when your Master shows up and you have to confess that you did nothing for him. Fix your heart on God with a steadfast confidence, and honor him with acts of heartfelt devotion.

OCTOBER 22

I will ... love them freely.
Hosea 14:4

This simple sentence is a powerful theology lesson. It capsulizes the glorious message of salvation that was given to us by Jesus Christ our Redeemer. If there were any way that we earned his love, that would diminish the freeness of it. But it stands: "I will love you freely." Remember, there are no conditions to the covenant of grace. Isn't it great to know that God's grace is utterly free to us.

OCTOBER 23

*You do not want to
leave too, do you?
John 6:67*

Many have forsaken Christ and have stopped walking with him. But what reason could *you* have to make such a change? When you have simply trusted Jesus, have you ever been let down? We have the joy of salvation – why give that up? Who trades gold for mud? We will never give up the sun until we find a better light, and we'll never leave our Lord until a brighter lover appears. And that will never happen.

OCTOBER 24

*The trees of the Lord
are well watered.
Psalm 104:16*

Without water, the tree cannot flourish – or even exist. In the same way, *vitality* is essential to a Christian. There must be *life* – the vital force infused into us by God's Holy Spirit. It is not enough to bear the name *Christian.* We must be filled with the spirit of divine life. With the tree, the water *eventually produces fruit.* So it is with a truly healthy Christian. There is so much of the life-giving Spirit within, that his whole being vibrates with divine power.

OCTOBER 25

Because of the truth, which lives in us and will be with us forever.
2 John 2

Once the truth of God enters the human heart and gets control of a person, nothing can dislodge it. We entertain it not as a guest, but as the master of our house. This is an essential part of the gospel. The truth will be with us forever. It will be a song in our hearts and our glory through all eternity.

OCTOBER 26

"You expected much, but see, it turned out to be little. What you brought home, I blew away. Why?" declares the Lord Almighty. "Because of my house, which remains a ruin, while each of you is busy with his own house."
Haggai 1:9

Stingy people cut back their contributions to church ministry and missionary support. Scripture teaches that the Lord enriches the one who gives freely and allows the miser to discover the sad result of his penny-pinching.

OCTOBER 27

Here is a trustworthy saying.
2 Timothy 2:11

Paul has four of these "trustworthy sayings". The first occurs in 1 Timothy 1:15: "Christ Jesus came into the world to save sinners." Others are: 1 Timothy 4:8, 2 Timothy 2:12 and Titus 3:7-8. Treasure these trustworthy sayings. Let them guide your life, comfort you, and teach you. They deserve full acceptance.

OCTOBER 28

I have chosen you out of the world.
John 15:19

Some of us are the special objects of divine affection. Don't be afraid to dwell on this doctrine of election. Those who doubt the doctrines of grace or prefer not to consider them are missing the choicest clusters of God's vineyard. Seek to enlarge your mind, so that you can comprehend more and more of the eternal love of God. Exult before the God of grace and leap with joy – because he has chosen you.

OCTOBER 29

This, then, is how you should pray: "Our Father in heaven."
Matthew 6:9

This prayer begins with the spirit of *adoption:* "Our Father"; ascends into *heartfelt adoration:* "hallowed be your name", to a *glowing missionary spirit:* "your kingdom come." Next is an *expression of dependence:* "Give us today our daily bread." Then you *beg for mercy:* "Forgive us our debts." You *ask for strength:* "Lead us not into temptation." Finally there is *triumphant praise:* "for yours is the kingdom and the power and the glory forever."

OCTOBER 30

I will praise you, O Lord.
Psalm 9:1

Praise should always follow answered prayer. Has the Lord been gracious to you? To be silent over God's mercies is to be guilty of ingratitude. Praise, like prayer, is one great way to develop our own spiritual life. It removes our burdens, excites our hope, increases our faith. Blessing God for the mercies we have received can also benefit those around us. Praise is the most heavenly of Christian duties.

OCTOBER 31

Renew a steadfast spirit within me.
Psalm 51:10

When a backslider is restored, the experience is similar to the original conversion. Repentance is required. We needed God's grace to come to Christ at first, and we need it to come back to him. No one can experience this renewal without the same burst of the Holy Spirit's energy that he felt at his conversion. Prayer is the method God uses to achieve his results. So pray often. Dwell on God's Word.

NOVEMBER

NOVEMBER 1

*The church that meets
in your home.
Philemon 2*

Is there a "church" in your home? Is there someone from your household or a friend of the family who needs to know Christ? Pray especially for that person this morning, that he or she would "return home", refreshing the hearts of all the saints (Philemon 7). You see, more is expected of a church than a mere household. Family worship must be more devout and exciting. Love within the home must be warm and unbroken.

NOVEMBER 2

I the Lord do not change.
Malachi 3:6

Despite all the changes in the world around us, there is One who never changes. This is the stability that an anchor gives a ship. It is the basis for Christian hope. God "does not change like shifting shadows" (James 1:17). His power, his wisdom, his justice, and his truth – all are unchanged. And his love never changes. He loves us now as much as he ever did. This gives us precious assurance.

NOVEMBER 3

For he is praying.
Acts 9:11

Prayers are instantly noticed in heaven. Often a brokenhearted person will get on his knees but can only utter his plea in the language of sighs and tears. Yet that groan makes all the harps of heaven vibrate with music. The tear is caught by God and treasured. Not only does God hear our prayers, but he *loves* to hear them. "He does not ignore the cry of the afflicted" (Psalm 9:12).

NOVEMBER 4

My power is made perfect in weakness.
2 Corinthians 12:9

A primary qualification for success in serving God is a sense of our own weakness. Those who serve God must serve him in God's way, in God's strength, or he will not accept their service. Whatever man does without God's help, God can never claim as his own. Are you bothered by your own weakness? Take courage, because there must be an awareness of weakness before the Lord gives you victory.

NOVEMBER 5

*No weapon forged
against you will prevail.
Isaiah 54:17*

The history of the church is full of examples of weapons forged against God's people. At first, the early Christians in Judea had to withstand opposition from their fellow Jews. For about 250 years, the Roman Empire had Christians arrested, tortured, and killed in savage ways. But even these horrendous methods did not prevail against Christ's church. "Take heart!" Jesus said. "I have overcome the world" (John 16:33). God's truth goes on.

NOVEMBER 6

*For I will pour water
on the thirsty land.
Isaiah 44:3*

Are you thirsting this morning for the living God? Are you depressed because the delight of God is missing from your heart? Then here is exactly the promise you need: "I will pour water on the thirsty land." You *will* receive the grace you need; you will have plenty. As water refreshes the thirsty, so grace will gratify your desires. As water awakens the sleeping plants, so a fresh supply of grace will awaken you.

NOVEMBER 7

See, I have engraved you on the palms of my hands.
Isaiah 49:16

There is an excitement in the word "see". It presents a way out of the doubting cry of verse 14: "But Zion said, 'The Lord has forsaken me.'" The Lord seems to be amazed at this unbelief. It should make us blush to hear the Lord's loving rebuke: "How can I forget you? I have engraved you on my hands!" He never fails. How could you ever think he has forgotten you?

NOVEMBER 8

*As you received
Jesus Christ as Lord.
Colossians 2:6*

The life of faith is a *receiving*. This implies the very opposite of any idea that we could earn our salvation. It is just the accepting of a gift. The idea of receiving implies a sense of *realization*. By an act of faith Jesus becomes a real person in our consciousness. But receiving also means *getting possession of*. The thing I receive becomes my own. When I receive Jesus, he becomes *my* Savior, so much mine that neither life nor death can rob me of him.

NOVEMBER 9

Continue to live in him.
Colossians 2:6

If we have received Christ into our innermost hearts, our new life will demonstrate our intimate acquaintance with him. The word for "live" in this verse is the word for "walk". The apostles pictured us walking through life *in Jesus*. If a person "walks" in Christ, he acts as Christ would act. We received Christ as Lord – he entered our lives through no merit of our own. But now we must "walk" *in him.*

NOVEMBER 10

The eternal God is your refuge.
Deuteronomy 33:27

The word "refuge" may also be translated "mansion" or "home", which yields a great new thought. *God is our home.* Home is precious, even if it's a humble cottage. Yet God is even more dear to us than that. At home we *feel safe.* At home, we *express ourselves freely.* We can communicate freely with God, speaking of all our hidden desires. Home is also the place of our *greatest happiness.* And in God we find our deepest delight.

NOVEMBER 11

*Underneath are
the everlasting arms.
Deuteronomy 33:27*

God – the eternal God – is *our support* at all times, especially when we are sinking in some deep trouble or concern. Sometimes a Christian sinks low in shame and humility. He has such a deep sense of his own sinfulness that he hardly knows how to pray. Sin may drag you down, but Christ's atonement still supports you. This assurance of support is a great comfort to those who are working hard in God's service.

NOVEMBER 12

*So that your faith ...
may be proved genuine.
1 Peter 1:7*

If faith is not tested, it may be true faith, but it will certainly be *small* faith. It will probably remain undersized until it is tested. Faith prospers most when things go against it. Storms are its teachers, and lightning just reveals its truths. But even if you can't claim the benefits of a lengthy experience of tested faith, thank God for the grace he gives you now.

NOVEMBER 13

No branch can bear fruit by itself.
John 15:4

How did you begin to bear fruit? It was when you came to Jesus, threw yourself on his great atonement, and rested on his righteousness. Some of us have to learn the hard way that all good things come from Christ. We reach a point of utter barrenness in our own lives before we realize how weak we really are. Then we simply depend again on the grace of God; we wait on the Holy Spirit; and the fruit returns.

NOVEMBER 14

*I will cut off from this place ...
those who bow down and
swear by the Lord and who
also swear by Molech.
Zephaniah 1:4-5*

Those people thought they were safe because they belonged to both parties. They worshiped with the followers of Yahweh, and they also bowed to Molech. But God hates such duplicity. He can't stand hypocrisy. My friend, search your own soul this morning. You profess to be a follower of Jesus – do you really love him? Is your heart right with God?

NOVEMBER 15

*For the Lord's portion
is his people.
Deuteronomy 32:9*

God's people are not only his by choice, but also *by purchase*. He has bought and paid for them, so there can be no disputing his claim. He bought them not with perishable things like silver and gold, but with the precious blood of Jesus (1 Peter 1:18-19). We have been chosen, bought, and won, and the Lord's rights to us are incontestable. So let us live each day to do his will and to show forth his glory.

NOVEMBER 16

I say to myself, "The Lord is my portion."
Lamentations 3:24

It is not, "The Lord is *partly* my portion." No, he makes up the sum total of my soul's inheritance. The *Lord* is my portion. Not only his grace or his love or his covenant, but Yahweh himself. When the Lord is our portion, we delight in him, who lets us drink freely from the river of his pleasures. Let us rejoice in him, showing the world how much God has blessed us.

NOVEMBER 17

To him be the glory forever! Amen.
Romans 11:36

This should be the greatest desire of any Christian. All other wishes must give way to this one. The Christian may want to improve his character, but only for the purpose of giving God glory. You should not be driven by any other motivation. Let God be your sole delight. If God has enriched you with experience, then praise him with a stronger faith than you had at first. If you have enjoyed happy times, then sing his praises more sweetly.

NOVEMBER 18

*A spring enclosed,
a sealed fountain.
Song of Songs 4:12*

This metaphor can apply to the inner life of the believer. First, we find the idea of *secrecy*. It is a spring *enclosed*. In biblical times there were springs that had buildings constructed over them, so that no one could get to them except those who knew the secret entrance. So is the heart of the believer, when it has been renewed by God's grace. There is a mysterious life within that no other human can touch.

NOVEMBER 19

But avoid foolish controversies.
Titus 3:9

It is better to spend our time doing good than arguing about things that are, at best, of minor importance. Our churches have suffered greatly from petty battles over obscure points and trivial questions. Wise believers avoid questions on points where Scripture is silent, on mysteries that belong to God alone, on prophecies of doubtful interpretation, and on methods of observing human rituals. We must follow the apostle's advice and devote ourselves to doing what is good (Titus 3:8).

NOVEMBER 20

O Lord, you took up my case.
Lamentations 3:58

Notice how positively the prophet speaks. He does not say, "I *hope*, I *trust*, I *sometimes think*, that God has taken up my case." No, he speaks of it as something that cannot be disputed. In the same way, we must shake off our doubts and see how gratefully the prophet speaks, giving all the glory to God alone. He doesn't credit any human effort with his redemption. No, it's "*you* took up my case; *you* redeemed my life." We should always be cultivating a grateful spirit.

NOVEMBER 21

And do not grieve the Holy Spirit.
Ephesians 4:30

All the believer has must come from Christ, but it comes only through the channel of the Holy Spirit. Just as all blessings come *to* you through the Spirit, so all good things that come *from* you are a result of the Spirit's sanctifying work in your life. Child of God, you have no life in you apart from the life God gives through his Spirit. So do not grieve the Spirit or make him angry by sinning against him. Be ready to obey every suggestion he offers.

NOVEMBER 22

Israel served to get a wife, and to pay for her he tended sheep.
Hosea 12:12

Jacob, arguing with Laban, described how hard he had worked. Our Savior's life on earth was even more difficult. He watched over all his sheep: "I have not lost one of those you gave me," he prayed (John 18:9). If Jesus had chosen to complain, he could have moaned louder than any underappreciated shepherd. His service was more exacting than anyone's. Like Jacob, he did it in order to win his bride.

NOVEMBER 23

Fellowship with him.
1 John 1:6

When we were united to Christ by faith, we were brought into fellowship with him. His interests and ours became mutual. We have fellowship with Christ in his *love*. What he loves, we love. We have fellowship with him in his *desires*. He desires God's glory – and we work toward the same goal. We also share Christ's *work*, ministering to people with words of truth and deeds of love.

NOVEMBER 24

There the Lord will be our Mighty One. It will be like a place of broad rivers and streams.
Isaiah 33:21

Broad rivers and streams produce fertile ground and abundant crops. That is what God does for his church. With God, the church has *abundance*. Is there anything the church could ask for that the Lord would not give her? He promises to supply all our needs. Do you crave the bread of life? It drops like manna from the sky. If you are in need, it is your own fault.

NOVEMBER 25

*To proclaim freedom
for the prisoners.
Luke 4:18*

No one but Jesus can offer freedom to prisoners. True freedom comes only from him. It is a freedom *righteously granted*. The Son, heir of all things, has the right to make people free. Our salvation occurs within the perfect justice of God. Our freedom has been *expensive to purchase*. Christ proclaims freedom with his powerful word, but he bought it with his blood. Although it has been costly, our freedom is *freely given*. Jesus asks nothing from us.

NOVEMBER 26

Whatever your hand finds to do, do it with all your might.
Ecclesiastes 9:10

"Whatever your hand finds to do" – this refers to actions that are *possible*. There are many things that our hearts want to do that will never come about. That is fine, but if we want to be truly effective, we should not be content with talking about the schemes of our hearts. Don't wait until your Christian experience has ripened into maturity – serve God *now*. When you serve him, do it with heart, soul, and strength (Mark 12:30).

NOVEMBER 27

Joshua the high priest standing before the angel of the Lord.
Zechariah 3:1

In Joshua the high priest, we see a picture of every child of God who has been brought to God by the blood of Christ and taught to serve the Lord in holiness. Jesus has made us priests and kings unto God, and even here on earth we exercise the priesthood of holy living and devoted service. But this high priest is described as "*standing* before the angel of the Lord", that is, standing to minister. This should be the position of every true believer.

NOVEMBER 28

It gave me great joy to have some brothers come and tell about your faithfulness to the truth and how you continue to walk in the truth.
3 John 3

The truth was in Gaius, and Gaius was in the truth. Truth must be a living force within us, an active energy, an indwelling reality. Walking in the truth, as Gaius did, involves a life of integrity, holiness, faithfulness, and simplicity.

NOVEMBER 29

"Do not go about spreading slander among your people ... Do not hate your brother in your heart. Rebuke your neighbor frankly so you will not share in his guilt."
Leviticus 19:16-17

Slander contains a triple-action poison. It harms the teller, the hearer, and the person who is slandered. Whether the report is true or false, God's Word tells us not to spread it. This should be our general rule: "to slander no one, to be peaceable and considerate, and to show true humility toward all men" (Titus 3:2).

NOVEMBER 30

Amaziah asked the man of God, "But what about the hundred talents I paid for these Israelite troops?" The man of God replied, "The Lord can give you much more than that."
2 Chronicles 25:9

This seemed to be a very important matter to King Amaziah. Maybe you can understand that. Losing money is never pleasant, and even when it is a matter of principle, we often find ourselves unwilling to make that sacrifice. We must obey God's will, and we can be sure that he will provide for us.

DECEMBER

DECEMBER 1

You made both summer and winter.
Psalm 74:17

If God is true to his Word in the revolving of the seasons, he will certainly prove faithful in his dealings with his own beloved Son. The winter of the soul is not a comfortable season at all. But this may comfort you: The Lord has made it. He sends the sharp blasts of adversity to nip the buds of expectation. Our Lord is a constant source of warmth and comfort in our times of trouble.

DECEMBER 2

All beautiful you are, my darling.
Song of Songs 4:7

The Lord's admiration for his church is wonderful. He describes her beauty in glowing terms. She is not merely "beautiful", but "*all* beautiful". He sees her in himself, washed in his atoning blood and clothed in his righteousness. He has written it in his Word and he sounds it forth even now. One day, from his glorious throne, he will confirm it. "Come, you who are blessed by my Father," he will say (Matthew 25:34).

DECEMBER 3

There is no flaw in you.
Song of Songs 4:7

The Lord has just announced how beautiful his church is. Now he adds a precious negative: "there is no flaw in you." Christ Jesus has no quarrel with his spouse. She often wanders from him, grieving his Holy Spirit, but he does not allow her faults to affect his love. He does not remember our foolish errors. He does not harbor grudges. He forgives us, and he loves us just as much after we sin as he does beforehand.

DECEMBER 4

I have many people in this city.
Acts 18:10

This should be a great motivation for us to take God's message to those around us. Among the people in your city – among the sinful, the degraded, the drunken – God has people whom he has chosen to save. When you take his Word to them, it means that God has chosen you to be the messenger of life to them. They must receive it, because God has chosen them to do so. The chosen moment has not yet come for them. But when it comes, they will obey.

DECEMBER 5

Ask and it will be given to you.
Matthew 7:7

Whenever a sinner is hungry, he only needs to knock, and his needs will be supplied. Whenever a soul is grimy and filthy, it can go there to be washed. Sinners have been washed whiter than snow (Isaiah 1:18). The sinner merely needs to ask, and he will be clothed. Knock there this morning and ask for large things from your generous Lord. Don't let unbelief hinder you. Jesus invites you. Jesus has promised to bless you. Don't hold back.

DECEMBER 6

As is the man from heaven, so also are those who are of heaven.
1 Corinthians 15:48

The body of Christ is all of one nature. Christ's mystical body is no absurd combination of opposites. Its members were mortal, so Jesus died. Isn't it amazing how Christ could humble himself to unite such wretched souls as ours? Yet he lifts us into a glorious union with himself. We are one with Christ! In comparison, all earthly honors are empty.

DECEMBER 7

He chose the lowly
things of this world.
1 Corinthians 1:28

Walk the streets by moonlight, if you dare, and you will see sinners then. Go wherever you want – you don't need to ransack the earth – sinners can be found everywhere, in every street of every city, town, village, and hamlet. Jesus died for these people. In God's supreme love, he has chosen to turn some of the worst into the best. This love doesn't care where you have been or what you have done. Just trust in him, and you will be saved.

DECEMBER 8

Yet you have a few people in Sardis who have not soiled their clothes. They will walk with me, dressed in white, for they are worthy.
Revelation 3:4

We may see this as *justification*. "They will walk with me, *dressed in white*." That is, they will enjoy a constant sense of being right with God. They will understand that the righteousness of Christ has been put on their account and that they have been washed, made whiter than the new-fallen snow.

DECEMBER 9

Therefore will the Lord wait that he may be gracious unto you.
Isaiah 30:18 KJV

God often delays in answering prayer. Our Father has his own reasons for keeping us waiting. Sometimes it is to show his power and sovereignty. More often, the delay is to our advantage. You may be kept waiting so that your desires will grow stronger. God knows that this will happen, and he may want you to see your need even more clearly, so you will appreciate his mercy, when it does come, all the more.

DECEMBER 10

And so we will be with the Lord forever.
1 Thessalonians 4:17

We can have occasional visits with Christ now, but oh, how short they are! We look forward eagerly to the time when we will see him not at a distance, but face-to-face. In heaven, our fellowship will not be interrupted by sin or by worries. We need not worry about the pain of death, because this sweet fellowship will make up for it. If dying means entering into uninterrupted communion with Jesus, then death truly is gain.

DECEMBER 11

The one who calls you is faithful and he will do it.
1 Thessalonians 5:24

Heaven is a place where we will never sin. The wicked will not trouble us, and we will be able to rest. Heaven is the land of perfect holiness and complete security. But don't we on earth sometimes taste a bit of this security? God's Word teaches us that all who are united to the Lamb are safe. I pray that God will convince you of your security in Christ. I pray that you will hear him whisper, "So do not fear, for I am with you" (Isaiah 41:10).

DECEMBER 12

His ways are eternal.
Habakkuk 3:6

Human ways are variable. But God's ways are eternal. Things that he has done he will do again. God is constant; he "does not change like shifting shadows" (James 1:17). His ways will always be the same. It is not only his might that gives stability; his ways are *the manifestation of the eternal principles of right.* Go to God this morning with confidence. He is gracious to his people, and that will never change.

DECEMBER 13

Salt without limit.
Ezra 7:22

Salt was used in every burnt offering made to the Lord. Due to its preserving and purifying properties, it became a symbol of God's grace in the soul. There is no limit on the salt of grace. So go to God's throne and get a large supply of heavenly salt. It will season your afflictions, preserve your heart, and kill your sins. You need a lot of it. Ask for it, and you'll get it.

DECEMBER 14

They go from strength to strength.
Psalm 84:7

These words convey the idea of progress. Those who rely on the Lord get stronger and stronger as they walk in the Lord's way. Usually, as we walk, we go from strength to weakness. But the Christian pilgrim obtains a fresh supply of grace along the way. He may not be quite as buoyant or bubbly; he may not burn with the same fiery zeal; but when it comes to real power, he is stronger that he ever was.

DECEMBER 15

Then Orpah kissed her mother-in-law good-bye, but Ruth clung to her.
Ruth 1:14

It is one thing to love the ways of the Lord when things are easy and quite another to cling to them when it's difficult. The kiss of outward respect is cheap and easy, but *clinging* to the Lord, making that decision for truth and holiness, is no trifling matter. Do not be satisfied this morning with a casual devotion to Christ. That is as empty as Orpah's kiss. By God's Holy Spirit, cling to Jesus.

DECEMBER 16

Come to me.
Matthew 11:28

This is the cry of the Christian religion: "Come." From the first moment of your spiritual life to the time you are ushered into glory, this is what Christ says to you: "Come, come to me." He goes before you to pave the way, to clear your path, and all your life you will hear his energizing voice. If you are a believer, you look forward to his second coming. "Come, Lord Jesus" (Revelation 22:20).

DECEMBER 17

*I remember the
devotion of your youth.
Jeremiah 2:2*

Christ loves to think about his church and to look on her beauty. We can never look too often on the face of someone we love. It is the same way with Jesus. From the beginning of time, he was "rejoicing in his whole world and delighting in mankind" (Proverbs 8:31). We may often forget to think of our Lord, but he never ceases to remember us.

DECEMBER 18

*Rend your heart and
not your garments.
Joel 2:13*

Garment rending and other outward signs of religious emotion are *easily done* and *frequently hypocritical.* True repentance is much more difficult – and much less common. This text commands us to rend our hearts, but that is not easy. Our hearts are naturally hard as marble. We must take them to Calvary. The voice of our dying Savior has split rocks before (Matthew 27:50-51). It is just as powerful now.

DECEMBER 19

The lot is cast into the lap, but its every decision is from the Lord.
Proverbs 16:33

If the Lord looks after even the casting of lots, don't you think he can arrange the events of your life? Remember that the Savior has said that even sparrows will not fall without our Father's will, and "even the very hairs of your head are all numbered" (Matthew 10:29-30). If he remembers sparrows, he won't forget you. "Cast your cares on the Lord and he will sustain you." (Psalm 55:22)

DECEMBER 20

*I have loved you with
an everlasting love.
Jeremiah 31:3*

Sometimes the Lord Jesus shares his loving thoughts with his people. He is wise enough to know when to hold back, but he often expresses his love clearly and announces it to the world. The Holy Spirit often confirms the love of Jesus, bearing witness with our spirit (Romans 8:16 KJV). He takes the things of Christ and reveals them to us. Listen to his sweet voice. Be assured that he loves you with an everlasting love.

DECEMBER 21

Has he not made with me an everlasting covenant?
2 Samuel 23:5

This covenant is *divine in its origin*. God has made it with us. Yes, God, the everlasting Father, stooped from his majesty, took hold of your hand, and made a covenant with you. Isn't that a remarkable deed? Can we ever really understand the humbling that was involved in that action? It would be incredible enough if a human king made an agreement with us. But the King of all kings – *he* has made an everlasting covenant with us.

DECEMBER 22

I will strengthen you.
Isaiah 41:10

God is certainly able to follow through on this promise. He has all the strength we need. The same God who keeps the earth in its orbit, who stokes the sun's furnace, who lights the stars of heaven, has promised to supply you with daily strength. O God, my strength, I believe in your promise. The limitless reservoir of your strength can never be exhausted. I can sing forever in your strength.

DECEMBER 23

Friend, move up to a better place.
Luke 14:10

When our Christian life first begins, we draw close to God, but only with fear and trembling. At that point the soul is very conscious of its guilt. But in later life, as we grow in grace, we lose that sense of terror. Our "fear" of God becomes a reverence, rather than a dread. We see not only his greatness, but his love, his goodness, his mercy. So we are invited to come to an even better position of closeness to God, rejoicing in him and crying, "Abba, Father."

DECEMBER 24

For your sakes he became poor.
2 Corinthians 8:9

The Lord Jesus Christ was eternally rich, glorified, and exalted. He could never have had fellowship with us unless he had shared with us his own abundant wealth, becoming poor to make us rich. If he had remained on his glorious throne and if we had stayed in the ruins of our sin, communion would have been impossible on both sides. *For your sake*, the Lord Jesus "became poor", so that he could lift you into communion with himself.

DECEMBER 25

The virgin will be with child and will give birth to a son, and will call him Immanuel.
Isaiah 7:14

The virgin birth was a thing previously unheard of and unparalleled since. The very first promise of the coming Savior referred to the seed of the woman (Genesis 3:15) and not to the offspring of man. Since the woman had led the way into sin, resulting in "Paradise Lost", it was fitting that she would bear the one to regain Paradise. Let us bow in reverence before this holy Child, whose innocence restores glory to humanity.

DECEMBER 26

The last Adam.
1 Corinthians 15:45

Jesus stands for every person he has chosen. Under the old agreement of works, Adam stood for every member of the human race. But under the new agreement of grace, every redeemed soul has a personal interest in Christ. We are one with him, since he is the Second Adam, the Sponsor of every chosen soul in this new covenant of love. Everything the Second Adam does is ours, too. Our salvation is based on this.

DECEMBER 27

*Can papyrus grow tall
where there is no marsh?
Job 8:11*

Papyrus is flimsy. So is the hypocrite. He has no substance or stability. The papyrus reed is shaken by every wind, just as the hypocrite yields to every outside influence. Is this your situation, too? Do you only serve God when it is profitable or respectable to do so? Those who follow Christ because they love him, these are the ones he loves in a special way.

DECEMBER 28

*The life I live in the body, I live
by faith in the Son of God.
Galatians 2:20*

Jesus' first command to us was "Live!" Life is absolutely essential in spiritual matters; until we have it, we have no way of participating in things of God's kingdom. What is this life that grace confers on us? It is none other than the life of Christ. Faith grabs hold of Jesus with a firm and determined grip. Christ Jesus is so delighted by faith that he keeps strengthening it and nurturing it in the believer, holding it in place with his eternal arms.

DECEMBER 29

Thus far has the Lord helped us.
1 Samuel 7:12

The phrase "thus far" is like a hand pointing to the past. Through poverty and wealth, in sickness and health, at home and abroad, "thus far has the Lord helped us!" But the phrase also points forward. When someone reaches a certain point and says, "Thus far," he is obviously not finished yet. There are more trials and joys. Thus far the Lord has proved himself faithful, but there is much, much more to come.

DECEMBER 30

*The end of a matter is
better than its beginning.
Ecclesiastes 7:8*

Look at our Lord's life. See how he began. "He was despised and rejected by men, a man of sorrows, and familiar with suffering" (Isaiah 53:3). But look how he ends up – at his Father's right hand, waiting in glory until his enemies are made his footstool (Luke 20:42-43). You are one of God's people. Let faith and patience fill your heart, for when your king is crowned, one perfect ray of glory will stream from you.

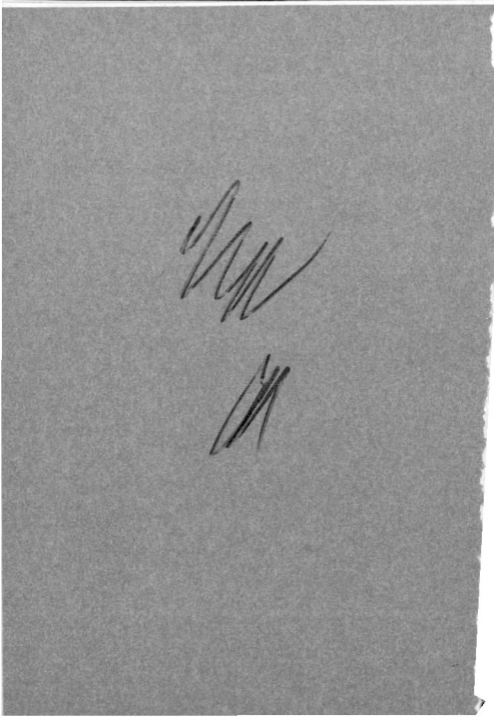